*FROM THE LIBRARY OF*

_____

_____

# MYSTERIES OF JOHN

## Also by Charles Fillmore

# MYSTERIES OF JOHN

## CHARLES FILLMORE

Unity Classic Library

**UNITY® Books**

**Unity Village, Missouri**

"Unity is a link in the great educational movement inaugurated by Jesus Christ; our objective is to discern the Truth and prove it. The Truth that we teach is not new, neither do we claim special revelations or discovery of new religious principles. Our purpose is to help and teach mankind to use and prove the eternal Truth taught by the Master."

—Charles Fillmore
Co-founder of Unity

*Mysteries of John* is a member of the
Unity Classic Library.

To receive a catalog of all Unity publications (books, cassettes, compact discs, and magazines) or to place an order, call the Customer Service Department: (816) 251-3580 or 1-800-669-0282. For information, address Unity Books, Publishers, Unity School of Christianity, 1901 NW Blue Parkway, Unity Village, MO 64065-0001.

First printing 1946; fourteenth printing 1997

Bible quotations in this book are from
the American Standard Version.

Marbled design by Mimi Schleicher © 1994
Cover design by Jill L. Ziegler

Library of Congress Catalog Card Number: 89-51143
ISBN 0-87159-204-5
Canada BN 13252 9033 RT

"The realization of divine unity is the highest that we can attain. This is true glory, the blending and merging of the whole being into Divine Mind.... This merging of God and man does not mean the total obliteration of man's consciousness but its glorification or expansion into that of the divine."

*Charles Fillmore*

# FOREWORD

ETAPHYSICAL BIBLE students recognize in the Gospel of John a certain spiritual quality that is not found in the other Gospels. Although this is not true of all Bible readers, it may be said that those who look for the mystical find it in the language of this book. The book is distinctive in this respect and is so successful in setting forth metaphysical truths that little interpretation is necessary. Only in a few instances does the original writing conceal the deep truths that the student seeks to discern. Written language is at best a reflection of inner ideas, and even though a teacher couples ideas and words as adroitly as Jesus does, elucidation is sometimes difficult.

Nevertheless ideas are catching, and this may be the best reason for publishing another book about this spirit-arousing Fourth Gospel. We are all heavily charged with ideas, and when these ideas are released they spring forth and pass from mind to mind, being "recorded" as they fly, and when they are expressed the whole race is lifted up—if the idea is charged with the uplifting Spirit. Jesus was God's idea of man made manifest in the flesh; so He was warranted in making that dynamic assertion, "I, if I be lifted up from the earth, will draw all men unto myself." Nowhere in all literature has this truth of the unity of God, man, and creation been so fearlessly expressed and affirmed by man as in the Book of John.

Here the question arises as to God's responsibility

for all that appears in the flesh, both good and evil, which seems to confound our logic and understanding. We are in human consciousness the fruit of a tree that stemmed from the soil of Being. The laws instituted in the aeons and ages of the past still prevail in the present. Interpreting Being from a personal standpoint, we have ignored the principles and laws at the very foundation of all creation and substituted a personal God, and many contradictions have followed. Now through the unfoldment of the spiritual man implanted in us in the beginning we are discerning the unchangeable laws of the good and the absolute necessity of conforming to them.

So we see that Jesus taught plainly that God functions in and through man and nature instead of being a person somewhere in the skies; also that we demonstrate God by making His Spirit manifest in our life. "He that hath seen me hath seen the Father." Socrates was asked, "What is a good man?" He replied, "A man who does good." Again he was asked, "What is good?" "What the good man does," he replied.

No extended definition of good is necessary to those who follow Jesus; even converted savages understand good and do it. The universal desire among awakened Christians to love God and man is part of the law constantly operating through man when he finds his right relation to God.

The status of evil is that of a parasite. It has no permanent life of itself; its whole existence depends on the life it borrows from its parent, and when its connection with the parent is severed nothing remains. Apparent evil is the result of ignorance, and when the truth is presented the error disappears. Jesus called it a liar and the father of lies.

Men personalize good and evil in a multiplicity of gods and devils, but Truth students follow Jesus in recognizing the supreme Spirit in man as the "one God and Father of all."

# CONTENTS

# John: Chapter 1

In the beginning was the Word, and the Word
was with God, and the Word was God. 2 The same
was in the beginning with God. 3 All things were
made through him; and without him was not anything made that hath been made. 4 In him was life;
and the life was the light of men. 5 And the light
shineth in the darkness, and the darkness appre-
hended it not.

IN PURE METAPHYSICS there is but one word, the
Word of God. This is the original creative
Word or thought of Being. It is the "God said"
of Genesis. The Greek original refers to it in the 1st
chapter of John as the *logos*. The Greek word cannot be adequately translated into English. In the
original it denotes wisdom, judgment, power, and in
fact all the inherent potentialities of Being. This
divine Logos was and always is in God; in fact
it is God as creative power. Divine Mind creates
under law; that is, spiritual law. Man may get a
comprehension of the creative process of Being by
analyzing the action of his own mind. First is mind,
then the idea in mind of what the act is to be, then
the act itself. Thus the Word and the divine process
of creating are identical.

Apart from mind nothing can be made. Even man,
in his forming and bringing anything into manifestation, uses the same creative process that God
used; to the degree that the qualities of the one
Mind enter into man's thought in the process his
work will be enduring.

The divine idea—the Christ or Word of God—
is always everywhere present.

Among the four Gospels that of John is readily discerned by metaphysicians as a symbolical life of Jesus and should appear first in the New Testament, corresponding to the first chapters of Genesis. Quite a few Bible critics so consider it, among them Ferrar Fenton, who gives it first place in his "Complete Bible in Modern English."

John explains that all existence is spiritual, that it comes to man as a gift, and that Christ is its fulfillment. "In the beginning was the Word, and the Word was with God, and the Word was God."

"The Word" is the English translation of the Greek *logos,* which means a thought or concept and also the word that is an expression or utterance of the same. It also involves the logical relation between idea and expression; hence our word logic, which also derives from *logos.*

Our attention is called to the 1st chapter of Genesis: "And the Spirit of God moved upon the face of the waters. And God said, Let there be light: and there was light."

Here in detail, day by day, or period by period, creation is ideated.

The parallel between Genesis and John is shown by the manifestation of the ideal man. In Genesis Adam appears first. In John it is John the Baptist, who is said to "bear witness" to the coming man, Jesus. In Genesis man was given dominion over all things; in John "all things were made through him."

John the Baptist represents the natural man, the physical man, who is the nucleus around which the spiritual man builds. Man may be compared to a house, the foundation being rock, the superstructure lighter material. The rock upon which Jesus built was not material: it was mental; its symbol, Peter, was a mind receptive to spiritual Truth and spiritual substance.

The first Adam was formed of the "dust of the ground," representing radiant substance instead of gross earth.

So John the Baptist was more than the perfect physical man. He was the illumined natural man. He preached and baptized his disciples and with spiritual vision saw the unfoldment of the natural man into the Christ man.

Spiritual man is the true light "which lighteth every man, coming into the world." The world was made by him and yet "knew him not."

There is a creative force constantly at work in man and all creation, but it is not recognized. It is Spirit-mind shining consciously in the minds and hearts of those who recognize it. Those who ignore this light do not "apprehend" it, and to them it is nonexistent.

"But as many as received him, to them gave he the right to become children of God, *even* to them that believe on his name."

> 6 There came a man, sent from God, whose name was John. 7 The same came for witness, that he might bear witness of the light, that all might believe through him. 8 He was not the light, but *came* that he might bear witness of the light.

Man in his darkened, ignorant state dwells in a realm of material thoughts and perceives nothing

higher until he arrives at the point in his unfoldment
where he is ready to receive understanding of the
Christ Truth. Then he enters into the John the
Baptist or intellectual perception of Truth. The intellectual perception of Truth by the natural man
(John the Baptist) is not the true light (the Christ)
but bears witness to the light and prepares the way
for its dawning in consciousness.

> 9 There was the true light, *even the light* which
> lighteth every man, coming into the world. 10 He
> was in the world, and the world was made through
> him, and the world knew him not. 11 He came unto
> his own, and they that were his own received him
> not.

The true light (the Christ or Word) that lights
every man coming into the world is and ever has
been in man. Even the outer man was formed and
came into existence through it. Up to a certain
stage in his unfolding man does not recognize this
truth; now however this mystery, which is "Christ in
you, the hope of glory," is being revealed to the
race with more and more clarity and with greatly
increased power.

> 12 But as many as received him, to them gave he
> the right to become children of God, *even* to them
> that believe on his name: 13 who were born, not of
> blood, nor of the will of the flesh, nor of the will of
> man, but of God.

According to the 12th and 13th verses, the same
truth that held good for Jesus will hold good for as

many as receive Him (the Christ) and believe in His resurrecting power as Jesus believed in it.

> 14 And the Word became flesh, and dwelt among us (and we beheld his glory, glory as of the only begotten from the Father), full of grace and truth.

Jesus recognized this truth that the Christ, the divine-idea man or Word of God, was His true self and that He was consequently the Son of God. Because Jesus held to this perfect image of the divine man, the Christ or Word entered consciously into every atom of His being, even to the very cells of His outer organism, and transformed all His body into pure, immortal, spiritual substance and life. Thus "the Word became flesh." The resurrecting of His whole being included His body. Jesus entered alive and entire into the spiritual realm.

> 15 John beareth witness of him, and crieth, saying, This was he of whom I said, He that cometh after me is become before me: for he was before me. 16 For of his fulness we all received, and grace for grace. 17 For the law was given through Moses; grace and truth came through Jesus Christ. 18 No man hath seen God at any time; the only begotten Son, who is in the bosom of the Father, he hath declared *him*.

"The law was given through Moses." Moses represents a phase of the evolutionary process in man. "The law"—the outer commandments—cannot redeem. "Grace and truth came through Jesus Christ"; that is, the real saving, redeeming, transforming power came to man through the work that Jesus did in establishing for the race a new and higher consciousness in the earth. We can enter into that consciousness by faith in Him and by means of the inner spirit of the law that He taught and practiced.

The 18th verse teaches that through the Christ in us we come into an understanding of the Father, since the Son (the Word) ever exists in God, and Father and Son are one and are omnipresent in man and in the universe. Spirit Truth is discerned through Spirit only; not in outer ways or through intellectual perception do we come to know God.

19 And this is the witness of John, when the Jews sent unto him from Jerusalem priests and Levites to ask him, Who art thou? 20 And he confessed, and denied not; and he confessed, I am not the Christ. 21 And they asked him, What then? Art thou Elijah? And he saith, I am not. Art thou the prophet? And he answered, No. 22 They said therefore unto him, Who art thou? that we may give an answer to them that sent us. What sayest thou of thyself? 23 He said, I am the voice of one crying in the wilderness, Make straight the way of the Lord, as said Isaiah the prophet. 24 And they had been sent from the Pharisees. 25 And they asked him, and said unto him, Why then baptizest thou, if thou art not the Christ, neither Elijah, neither the prophet? 26 John answered them, saying, I baptize in water: in the midst of you standeth one whom we know not, 27 *even* he that cometh after me, the latchet of whose shoe I am not worthy to unloose. 28 These things were done in Bethany beyond the Jordan, where John was baptizing.

In the regeneration two states of mind are constantly at work. First comes the cleansing or denial state, in which all the error thoughts are eliminated. This includes forgiveness for sins committed and a general clearing up of the whole consciousness. The idea is to get back into the pure, natural consciousness of Spirit. This state of mind is typified by John the Baptist, who came out of the wilderness a child of nature whose mission it was to make straight the way for One who was to follow.

This putting away of sin from the consciousness (baptism through denial, plus forgiveness) is very closely allied to the deeper work that is to follow; so much so that to the observer it seems the same. Hence the followers of John, when they saw the works he did, asked if he was the Messiah. His answer was that the One who followed him was to baptize with Holy Spirit.

From this we discern that mental cleansing and the reforms that put the conscious mind in order are designed to prepare the way for that larger and more permanent consciousness which is to follow. This is the denial of "self" or personality. Jesus said, "If any man would come after me, let him deny himself." We are all guilty in a way of undue devotion to personal aims, which are always narrow and selfish. So long as these exist and take the place of the rightful One there is no room for the higher self, the Christ of God.

The recorded "This is the Son of God" is a reference to a matter of first importance in the regeneration. The recognition of man as the Son of God and the establishment in the mind of the

new relations between the divine Father and the
Son are essential to the process. If we do not affirm
our sonship, with all its privileges and powers, we
are sure to belittle ourselves and make limitations
that prevent us from entering into the fullness of the
Godhead. "Be perfect, as your heavenly Father is
perfect."

> 29 On the morrow he seeth Jesus coming unto
> him, and saith, Behold, the Lamb of God, that taketh
> away the sin of the world! 30 This is he of whom I
> said, After me cometh a man who is become before
> me: for he was before me. 31 And I knew him not;
> but that he should be made manifest to Israel, for
> this cause came I baptizing in water. 32 And John
> bare witness, saying, I have beheld the Spirit de-
> scending as a dove out of heaven; and it abode upon
> him. 33 And I knew him not; but he that sent me to
> baptize in water, he said unto me, Upon whomsoever
> thou shalt see the Spirit descending, and abiding upon
> him, the same is he that baptizeth in the Holy Spirit.
> 34 And I have seen, and have borne witness that this
> is the Son of God.

Metaphysically interpreted, John the Baptist symbolizes in each individual the natural man, but with
an illumined intellect. His face is turned toward the
light in the measure that he recognizes and pays
homage to the higher self within the individual. John
baptized with water all those who believed that
Jesus was soon to make His appearance. This is a
cleansing, purifying process, preparing the individual to see spiritually and to discern spiritually.

The Father-Mind is the living principle, the

absolute, the unlimited. The Son is the living Word.
"Word" is used to designate man's I AM identity.
The Holy Spirit is the action or outpouring or activ-
ity of the living Word. This activity produces what
may be termed the light of Spirit, the breath of God,
the "personality" of Being. The outpouring of the
Holy Spirit is the sign by which the natural man rec-
ognizes the divine. Jesus, who became the "Lamb of
God" or perfect expression of God, baptized in the
Holy Spirit.

> 35 Again on the morrow John was standing, and
> two of his disciples; 36 and he looked upon Jesus as
> he walked, and saith, Behold, the Lamb of God!

By cultivation the spiritual mind becomes an active factor in consciousness. It has to be desired and
sought before it becomes a part of one's conscious
life. John the Baptist (the natural conscious mind)
is expecting, looking for, and earnestly desiring a
greater realization of Spirit. He knows that he is not
fulfilling the Christ ideal of manhood; hence his
prophecy of One who is to come, "the latchet of
whose shoe" he is not worthy to loose.

This willingness to give up the natural man to
the divine is a most propitious sign in one who is in
the regenerative process. Many persons are ambitious
to put on Christ, but are not willing to give up the
present man in order to do so. John the Baptist had a
following, yet he was willing that his disciples should
go to Jesus. He openly acknowledged Him as the
"Lamb of God." This was his acknowledgment of
the Christ Mind. That mind has no personal ambi-

tion; it is innocent, loving, and obedient to the call of God.

> 37 And the two disciples heard him speak, and they followed Jesus. 38 And Jesus turned, and beheld them following, and saith unto them, What seek ye? And they said unto him, Rabbi (which is to say, being interpreted, Teacher), where abidest thou? 39 He saith unto them, Come, and ye shall see. They came therefore and saw where he abode; and they abode with him that day: it was about the tenth hour. 40 One of the two that heard John *speak,* and followed him, was Andrew, Simon Peter's brother. 41 He findeth first his own brother Simon, and saith unto him, We have found the Messiah (which is, being interpreted, Christ). 42 He brought him unto Jesus. Jesus looked upon him, and said, Thou art Simon the son of John: thou shalt be called Cephas (which is by interpretation, Peter).

When the conscious mind recognizes the Christ Mind, the various faculties gradually awaken and attach themselves to it. Andrew is the first apostle mentioned, and with him was one whose name is not given here but who is supposed to have been John (love). Love is modest and retiring, "seeketh not its own." Andrew represents the strength of the mind, which, greatly rejoiced when it finds the inexhaustible source of all strength, exclaims, "We have found the Messiah."

Strength is clearly related to substance (Simon), which in spirit we call faith. "Faith is the substance of things hoped for" (A.V.). What we hope for and mentally see as a possibility in our life comes into visibility, and we call it substantial.

43 On the morrow he was minded to go forth into Galilee, and he findeth Philip: and Jesus saith unto him, Follow me. 44 Now Philip was from Bethsaida, of the city of Andrew and Peter. 45 Philip findeth Nathanael, and saith unto him, We have found him, of whom Moses in the law, and the prophets, wrote, Jesus of Nazareth, the son of Joseph. 46 And Nathanael said unto him, Can any good thing come out of Nazareth? Philip saith unto him, Come and see. 47 Jesus saw Nathanael coming to him, and saith of him, Behold, an Israelite indeed, in whom is no guile! 48 Nathanael saith unto him, Whence knowest thou me? Jesus answered and said unto him, Before Philip called thee, when thou wast under the fig tree, I saw thee. 49 Nathanael answered him, Rabbi, thou art the Son of God; thou art King of Israel. 50 Jesus answered and said unto him, Because I said unto thee, I saw thee underneath the fig tree, believest thou? thou shalt see greater things than these. 51 And he saith unto him, Verily, verily, I say unto you, Ye shall see the heaven opened, and the angels of God ascending and descending upon the Son of man.

The name *Philip* means "lover of horses," and Philip is symbolic of the vigor, power, vitality, and energy of the mind. Philip, Andrew, and Peter are of the same "city," Bethsaida. The name *Bethsaida* means "house of fishing," and Bethsaida signifies a group of thoughts in consciousness that have as their central idea a belief in the increase of ideas and their expression and manifestation in outer form.

Nathanael (representing the imagination) is also called Bartholomew. In the realm of the real (Israel) the imaging power of the mind is guileless, innocent of error images. It is open and receptive to the beauty and perfection of Being. It is the faculty of imagination that makes the great artist and the great poet. It is the guileless innocence of the Nathanael state of mind that causes the religious enthusiast to believe all things about Spirit and the world invisible. Exercised without Christ understanding, the imagination becomes delusory. It is the image maker in the psychic; the clairvoyant may be deceived by its conjuring power. In itself it is not error, but it may, like all the other faculties, be used in erroneous ways. When the Mind of Spirit uses it, as in the case of Jesus' discerning Nathanael when he was under the fig tree, it is without guile; and in God's communication with man this faculty plays an important part.

Among the apostles, Bartholomew represents the imagination. He is called Nathanael in the 1st chapter of John, where it is recorded that Jesus saw him under the fig tree, the inference being that He discerned Nathanael's presence before the latter came into visibility. This would indicate that images of people and things are projected into the imaging chamber of the mind and that by giving them attention one can understand their relation to outer things. Mind readers, clairvoyants, and dreamers have developed this capacity to varying degree. Consciousness is what is concerned with soul unfoldment both primarily, and secondarily and all the way! Forms are always manifestations of ideas. Whoever understands this can interpret the symbols shown him in dreams and visions, but lack of understanding of this law makes one a psychic without discernment.

With this spiritual faculty it is possible for man to penetrate into the "fourth dimension" or what is usually called the "kingdom of the heavens" and to discern the trend of the spiritual forces. The angels of God are spiritual forces active in the Sons of God, the spiritually quickened.

The open and receptive and believing mind can see the things that take place in the Christ Mind, thus transcending the capacity of the unillumined natural man.

# John: Chapter 2

And the third day there was a marriage in Cana of Galilee; and the mother of Jesus was there: 2 and Jesus also was bidden, and his disciples, to the marriage. 3 And when the wine failed, the mother of Jesus saith unto him, They have no wine. 4 And Jesus saith unto her, Woman, what have I to do with thee? mine hour is not yet come. 5 His mother saith unto the servants, Whatsoever he saith unto you, do it. 6 Now there were six waterpots of stone set there after the Jews' manner of purifying, containing two or three firkins apiece. 7 Jesus saith unto them, Fill the waterpots with water. And they filled them up to the brim. 8 And he saith unto them, Draw out now, and bear unto the ruler of the feast. And they bare it. 9 And when the ruler of the feast tasted the water now become wine, and knew not whence it was (but the servants that had drawn the water knew), the ruler of the feast calleth the bridegroom, 10 and saith unto him, Every man setteth on first the good wine; and when *men* have drunk freely, *then* that which is worse: thou hast kept the good wine until now. 11 This beginning of his signs did Jesus in Cana of Galilee, and manifested his glory; and his disciples believed on him.

SPIRITUALLY A marriage represents the union of two dominant states of consciousness. Mary, the mother of Jesus, represents intuition, the spiritual soul, Eve, "the mother of all living." Jesus is the personal I AM and His apostles are the twelve faculties.

Cana is a "place of reeds"; so is the larynx found in the body. The name Galilee means "to whirl"; air is rapidly forced through the larynx in speaking or singing. The apostles represent the dominant nerve centers, the spiritual symbolism of each being concealed in the name. Philip means "one who is fond of horses." The horse symbolizes vigor, vitality, power. Vigor or its opposite, weakness, is betrayed by the voice, so we designate Philip as the power faculty, and his place in body expression is in the larynx (at Cana).

Water may be compared to natural or human life, and wine to spiritual life. In the regeneration spirit and body are united, but before this union can be accomplished the exhausted natural life must be quickened with spirit (symbolized by the turning of water into wine). This lack of vitalizing life is first realized by Mary, the source of all life, but Jesus, the directive I AM in all bodily activities, does not feel that He is yet ready to perform this seeming miracle and pleads delay: "Mine hour has not yet come."

But the urge of the inner forces is strong and the confident mother is sure that her son can do all things: "Whatsoever he saith unto you, do it."

The water pots filled to the brim with water by the servants represent the extent to which nature is prepared to fulfill the transformation from negative life to spiritual life through the power of the word of the Master, Jesus: "Draw out now, and bear to the ruler of the feast." The ruler of the feast, the supreme I AM, pronounced the transformed water to be superior to the best wine.

This transformation of the negative, watery fluid of the organism into vitalizing Spirit is accomplished by adding to every word a spiritual idea. The idea of omnipresent life will then quicken the natural life

in man, and it will make conscious contact with the
one life and draw it out for the benefit of the many.

When the I is "lifted up" there is a higher vital
action imparted to the whole consciousness. Jesus
said, "I, if I be lifted up from the earth, will draw all
men unto myself." The lifting up of the I is the result
of spiritual perception of Truth. When we discern
the real truth of being and our relation to it, there is
a new and higher consciousness established. This
greater energy is first imparted to the soul or thought
realm and through it to the body. This whole process
is under law. There is a definite consecutive connection of thought and thing, through laws that
may be discerned by man and used universally. At
the close of chapter 1, Jesus had caught sight of the
spiritual realm and said: "Ye shall see the heaven
opened, and the angels of God ascending and descending upon the Son of man."

This high perception of man's union, through
the I AM, with the divine harmony sets up a sym-
pathetic vibration that is imparted to every part of
consciousness. The marriage that took place in Cana
of Galilee symbolizes this union in which the negative watery elements of the body were "lifted up"
to wine or Spirit. A Bible authority says that His
remark is more correctly stated in the words: "Woman, what is there between me and thee?" This
interrogation depicts the questioning attitude of the
personal I AM, Jesus. It is not clear in its understanding of what is to be done. It is looking forward
to a time when it will act, but its "hour is not yet
come." We find ourselves wanting to see all the

steps of our actions before we begin, but in spiritual processes we have to proceed without foreknowing the various steps. If we go ahead and speak the word, the law will see us through. The elemental forces of Being (servants) are at hand to carry out our orders, and the intuitive perfection of Truth (woman) within us commands that those forces do our bidding.

The symbolism of this miracle has to do with the abundance of vital energy that may be generated from a union of man with the "water of life" or nerve substance in the various centers of his organism. With every thought we are putting the nerve substance into a state of action, and it rushes to any part of the body that is the center of attention. When we have been much excited or interested there is a concentration of vitality in the head, and if we do not know how to restore and equalize this vitality again in the body, we have a headache or the stuffy condition called a cold. To equalize: Center the attention in the larynx and declare, "All equalizing, harmonizing power is given unto me in mind and body."

In regeneration there is a permanent transmutation of physical vitality into higher consciousness, and a new element is introduced into the organism. "The ruler of the feast" (the Lord) praises the transmuted substance as the best offered at the wedding feast.

12 After this he went down to Capernaum, he, and his mother, and *his* brethren, and his disciples; and there they abode not many days.

Capernaum designates or represents an inner conviction of the abiding compassion and restoring power of Being. When one enters this state of consciousness a healing virtue pours out of the soul and transforms all discord into harmony.

Jesus and His mother and His brethren and His disciples went into this state of consciousness.

13 And the passover of the Jews was at hand, and Jesus went up to Jerusalem.

It is the nature of thought to repeat itself. At each repetition it will grow stronger or weaker as it is consciously recognized or ignored by man. Thus we can cultivate a good movement of the mind by giving it a special affirmation (feast). The Feast of the Passover that Jesus went up to Jerusalem to attend symbolizes an escape from bondage. When we begin to discipline our mind we always go up in consciousness, because it is from our spiritual height that we see things clearly and in their right relation.

14 And he found in the temple those that sold oxen and sheep and doves, and the changers of money sitting.

When we throw the light of Spirit into the subconscious courts of the body temple, we find queer and often startling conditions there. One would hardly expect to see butcher stalls and money-changers in a temple built for the worship of God, yet similar conditions exist in all of us.

15 And he made a scourge of cords, and cast all out of the temple, both the sheep and the oxen; and

he poured out the changers' money, and overthrew their tables; 16 and to them that sold doves he said, Take these things hence; make not my Father's house a house of merchandise.

So the body temple must be cleansed; it is the house of God ("for we are a temple of the living God"), and it should be put in order. The first step in this cleansing process is to recognize its need. The next step is the "scourge of small cords" (A.V.): to formulate the word or statement of denial. When we deny in general terms we cleanse the consciousness, but secret sins may yet lurk in the inner parts. The words that most easily reach these hidden errors are not great ones, such as "I am one with Almightiness; my environment is God" but small, definite statements that cut like whipcords into the sensuous, fleshly mentality.

To get perfect results it is necessary to deal with our mind in both the absolute and the relative. In the early morning we may affirm, *"All the affairs of my life are under the law of justice, and my own comes to me in ways divine,"* and before noon find ourselves searching the papers for advertisements of bargains in the stores. Such an experience shows that we have not gone into the temple and tipped over the tables and scattered the coins.

17 His disciples remembered that it was written, Zeal for thy house shall eat me up.

Excessive zeal in observing the forms of religious worship eats up the truly spiritual. "The zeal of thine house hath eaten me up." When we become very zealous in observing the rites of the church, we are prone to forget the church itself, which is Christ.

The light of Jesus Christ is, symbolically, the life of everyone who enters the same state of mind that He did. You always reap the consequences of your thought, and to enter the Christ Mind you have but to think along Jesus Christ lines.

Every man produces a thought atmosphere that has character and power in proportion to his ability as a thinker. Power increases with expansion; in thought, power is great or small as the ideals are high or low. When you follow narrow ideals your thought atmosphere is correspondingly contracted; but mental breadth enlarges and strengthens it in all directions.

"How can a man conceal himself?" said Confucius. In the light of the ever-present thought atmosphere with which we surround ourselves, he cannot. Nearly all people have the ability of sensing the thought atmosphere of those they meet; and a man may cultivate this ability to project himself until he becomes an open book and the air about him is filled with his silent yet potent words, ever telling what he has thought.

The thought atmosphere is a real, substantial thing, and has in it all that makes the body. We have a way of considering the things we cannot see as unsubstantial, and although we are told that we cannot conceal ourselves we go right on believing that we can. Hence it is good for us to know that of a truth we do carry about with us this open book of our life, out of which all persons read whether we realize it or not. Some people are good thought readers while others are dull, but all can read a little, and you cannot conceal yourself. Also your thought atmosphere is constantly printing its slowly cooling words on your body, where they are seen of men. But with a little practice we can feel the thought force of this atmosphere that surrounds us and gradually gain a realization of its existence that is as real as that of the outer world.

"Think on these things," said Paul. Think about Christ as a life force penetrating your whole being. Try to feel this force as an energy pulsating through every nerve and fiber of your body. Then imagine you can see this life force as a light lighting up every cell. Light represents intelligence, and when the light in you breaks forth into understanding you will know that there is a spiritual mind that is as much greater than the ordinary mind as the sun is greater than the moon. In Him is life, and this life is the light of men.

18 The Jews therefore answered and said unto him, What sign showest thou to us, seeing that thou doest these things? 19 Jesus answered and said unto them, Destroy this temple, and in three days I will raise it up. 20 The Jews therefore said, Forty and six years was this temple in building, and wilt thou raise it up in three days? 21 But he spake of the temple of his body. 22 When therefore he was raised from the dead, his disciples remembered that he spake this; and they believed the scripture, and the word which Jesus had said.

That the temple referred to means the body is

clearly stated in verse 21: "But he spake of the temple of his body." Man's ability to preserve his body from destruction is the proof that he has mastered his mind. So long as our body shows signs of decay it is evident that we have not cast out of the inner realms the "thought butchers" that for a sacrifice kill doves, sheep, oxen, and goats. The allusion here is to the destructive thoughts lying deep in the consciousness at the very issues of life.

The "three days" are spirit, soul, and body, the three "degrees" or parts of man's consciousness. When the I AM of man has purified and mastered these three, man is in the dominion proclaimed for him in the 1st chapter of Genesis; the Scripture or Word of God is fulfilled in him, and his faculties (disciples) recognize and respond to it every time that the uplifting word (the resurrecting word) is proclaimed.

> 23 Now when he was in Jerusalem at the passover, during the feast, many believed on his name, beholding his signs which he did. 24 But Jesus did not trust himself unto them, for that he knew all men, 25 and because he needed not that any one should bear witness concerning man; for he himself knew what was in man.

Truth is of the absolute order and does not have to be proved. Jesus recognized this fact and therefore did not feel it necessary to place any great value on the opinion of those who had not yet fully attained spiritual consciousness.

# John: Chapter 3

Now there was a man of the Pharisees, named Nicodemus, a ruler of the Jews: 2 the same came unto him by night, and said to him, Rabbi, we know that thou art a teacher come from God; for no one can do these signs that thou doest, except God be with him.

THIS 3d chapter of John opens with a narrative of Nicodemus, "a ruler of the Jews," his visit to Jesus "by night" (meaning the darkness of intellectual understanding), and his confession: "Thou art a teacher from God; for no one can do these signs that thou doest, except God be with him."

Jesus told him that he must be "born anew," "of water and the Spirit." Here is a recognition by the Master of the operation of the divine law of evolution.

All "inheritance" of ideas and beliefs has a mental basis. We "inherit" some states of mind from our ancestors. An "inherited" or transmitted religion is a dark state, if there is no real understanding in it. This is the Nicodemus mentality. Nicodemus was a Pharisee and a ruler of the Jews. He represents the Pharisaical side of our mentality that observes the external forms of religion without understanding their real meaning. We accept our parents' religious affiliations without giving any thought to their origin. There was a time when it was considered unfilial and an evidence of disobedience for the children to join any other church than that to which their parents belonged. The Jews

were especially rigid in their adherence to their
traditional religion, and they proudly referred to
their fathers Abraham, Isaac, and Jacob, who were
taught of God.

This conservative religious thought preserves the
church as an institution and restrains the individual
from becoming religiously erratic. Nicodemus was a
friend of Jesus', but his defense of the Master was
put in the form of a question, reminding the San-
hedrin of the Jewish law that every man must be
heard or given a chance to defend himself before
being condemned. The "ruler of the Jews" did not
press his championship of his friend before the San-
hedrin, and the assistance that he gave at the tomb
of Jesus was safe enough, once the prosecutors and
executioners had finished their work and turned
their attention elsewhere.

Nicodemus was not acquainted with the power of
Spirit and really had no understanding of regeneration, although he was a "teacher of Israel" (Israel
representing thoughts that pertain to the religious
department of the mind).

3 Jesus answered and said unto him, Verily, verily,
I say unto thee, Except one be born anew, he cannot
see the kingdom of God. 4 Nicodemus saith unto
him, How can a man be born when he is old? can he
enter a second time into his mother's womb, and be
born? 5 Jesus answered, Verily, verily, I say unto
thee, Except one be born of water and the Spirit, he
cannot enter into the kingdom of God. 6 That which
is born of the flesh is flesh; and that which is born of
the Spirit is spirit. 7 Marvel not that I said unto thee,
Ye must be born anew. 8 The wind bloweth where it

will, and thou, hearest the voice thereof, but knowest
not whence it cometh, and whither it goeth: so is
every one that is born of the Spirit.

The Pharisees refused to be baptized by John.
They did not consider that they needed the re-
pentance that he demanded. They thought they were
good enough to take the high places in the kingdom
of God because of their popularly accepted religious
supremacy. Many people refuse to deny their short-
comings. They hold that they are perfect in Divine
Mind and that it is superfluous to deny that which
has no existence. But they are still subject to the ap-
petites and passions of mortality, and will continue
to be until they are "born anew."

The new birth is an uncertainty to the intellectual
Christian, hence there has gradually evolved a popular belief that after death the souls of those who have
accepted the church creed and have been counted
Christians will undergo a change. But in His instruc-
tions to Nicodemus Jesus makes no mention of a
resurrection after death as having any part in the
new birth. He cites the ever present though unseen
wind as an illustration of those who are born of
Spirit. The new birth is a change that comes here and
now. It has to do with the present man, that he may
be conscious of the "Son of man," who is the real I
AM in each individual. "And no one hath ascended
into heaven, but that descended out of heaven, *even*
the Son of man, who is in heaven."

This chapter of John contains some of the vital
truths taught in Christianity: the evolution of man
from natural to spiritual consciousness, and the in-

carnation of Jesus Christ as the divine pattern for all
men who are seeking the way of life.

Christianity teaches the complete law of evolution as compared with the partial exposition of the
law made by Darwin and associates. Christianity
describes God as Spirit creating by a process com-
parable to the mental processes with which we are all
familiar. "God said," and thus God created that
which was to appear, God planned man and the universe, and through His word projected them into
creation as ideal principles and immanent energies
acting behind and within all visibility. But we should
remember that Spirit could not emerge from the
formless into the formed without creating relations,
which necessitated laws operating through man and
all things as essential factors in an orderly universe.
Thus even God becomes subject to His laws or commandments. God the universal Spirit first appears as
spiritual man. The next step in evolution is the appearance of the idea of spiritual man in the natural
or Adam man. This man was primitively identified
with an infinite capacity for expansion. When he
recognizes his identity as being that of his source,
Spirit, he expands in divine order and brings forth
only good. When he deserts his spiritual anchorage
and gives attention to external experiences and sen-
sations, he falls into a world in which a diversity of
results obtain that he calls good and evil. Thus man
eats "of the fruit of the tree of the knowledge of good
and evil." In these few words is summed up the fall
of man from an Edenic state, where he had the
constant inspiration of creative Mind, to a con-

sciousness of matter and the desperate struggle of personality for existence.

The natural man must evolve into the spiritual. "And as Moses lifted up the serpent in the wilderness, even so must the Son of man be lifted up."

We are told here that "the light is come into the world, and men loved the darkness rather than the light." World chaos results from the lack of spiritual light. We may plan peace and achieve it, but if this peace is not based on divine law, evolving love, and that law incorporated into the pact of peace as well as into the minds of those who sign that pact, we shall have no permanent peace.

> 9 Nicodemus answered and said unto him, How can these things be?

There is but one real man, the ideal or spiritual man that God created. Jesus was explaining to Nicodemus the evolution of this spiritual man from his ideal to his manifest state. Man is fundamentally spiritual and so remains throughout his various manifestations. He comes out of heaven, manifests himself as a personality in the earth, and returns to heaven. The first Adam was in Paradise, and after his fall enough of his spiritual nature remained to keep him alive. Without this animating Spirit the whole human family would have perished with the fall of Adam. Faith in Spirit and the ultimate dominance of the good in man will finally restore him to the heaven from which he descended.

The new birth is simply the realization by man of

his spiritual identity, with the fullness of power and glory that follows.

> 10 Jesus answered and said unto him, Art thou the teacher of Israel, and understandest not these things? 11 Verily, verily, I say unto thee, We speak that which we know, and bear witness of that which we have seen; and ye receive not our witness. 12 If I told you earthly things and ye believe not, how shall ye believe if I tell you heavenly things? 13 And no one hath ascended into heaven, but he that descended out of heaven, *even* the Son of man, who is in heaven. 14 And as Moses lifted up the serpent in the wilderness, even so must the Son of man be lifted up; 15 that whosoever believeth may in him have eternal life.
>
> 16 For God so loved the world, that he gave his only begotten Son, that whosoever believeth on him should not perish, but have eternal life. 17 For God sent not the Son into the world to judge the world; but that the world should be saved through him.

"For God so loved the world, that he gave his only begotten Son, that whosoever believeth on him [His own divine self] should not perish, but have eternal life." Not only are we to believe in our own divinity, but we are to accept the example of that divinity expressed through Jesus Christ.

To believe in Jesus is to believe that in the regenerate state we are to be, like Him, "joint-heirs with Christ." This belief must then lead us to a desire and an effort to attain our inheritance, because then we know that there is no other thing in the universe worth striving for. Every person in his real, true self desires to be just as great and just as good as it is possible for him to be. The open door to the attainment of this objective is to believe in one's own divinity and then to raise oneself to its level by following the example of Jesus.

This text reveals the heart of the glad tidings of Jesus Christ to mankind. In love God gave His only-begotten Son, the fullness of the perfect-man idea in Divine Mind, the Christ, to be the true, spiritual self of every individual. By following Jesus' example of recognizing and acknowledging the Christ in our every thought, word, and deed, thus unifying ourselves with His completeness, the outer will become as the inner; we shall be like Christ; we shall know Him as He is. He who truly believes "cometh not into judgment, but hath passed out of death into life."

18 He that believeth on him is not judged: he that believeth not hath been judged already, because he hath not believed on the name of the only begotten Son of God. 19 And this is the judgment, that the light is come into the world, and men loved the darkness rather than the light; for their works were evil. 20 For every one that doeth evil hateth the light, and cometh not to the light, lest his works should be reproved. 21 But he that doeth the truth cometh to the light, that his works may be made manifest, that they have been wrought in God.

Salvation from the results of error thought begins at once when we have faith in the power of the Lord Jesus Christ to save us from the judgment. He comes to us in Spirit to do away with the effects of transgression of the law. When we perceive the way of righteousness and Truth and follow it, there comes to us a new light, an understanding of the law, and we enter the kingdom of God here and now. *"Even the Son of man, who is in heaven."*

22 After these things came Jesus and his disciples into the land of Judæa; and there he tarried with them, and baptized. 23 And John also was baptizing in Ænon near to Salim, because there was much water there: and they came, and were baptized. 24 For John was not yet cast into prison. 25 There arose therefore a questioning on the part of John's disciples with a Jew about purifying. 26 And they came unto John, and said to him, Rabbi, he that was with thee beyond the Jordan, to whom thou hast borne witness, behold, the same baptizeth, and all men come to him. 27 John answered and said, A man can receive nothing, except it have been given him from heaven. 28 Ye yourselves bear me witness, that I said, I am not the Christ, but, that I am sent before him. 29 He that hath the bride is the bridegroom: but the friend of the bridegroom, that standeth and heareth him, rejoiceth greatly because of the bridegroom's voice: this my joy therefore is made full. 30 He must increase, but I must decrease.

31 He that cometh from above is above all: he that is of the earth is of the earth, and of the earth he speaketh: he that cometh from heaven is above all. 32 What he hath seen and heard, of that he beareth witness; and no man receiveth his witness. 33 He that hath received his witness hath set his seal to *this,* that God is true. 34 For he whom God hath sent speaketh the words of God: for he giveth not the Spirit by measure. 35 The Father loveth the Son, and hath given all things into his hand. 36 He that believeth on the Son hath eternal life; but he that obeyeth not the Son shall not see life, but the wrath of God abideth on him.

Jesus represents the Christ. Judea represents praise. John the Baptist and Jesus represent co-operation between the intellect and the Spirit.

Metaphysically interpreted, John the Baptist represents the intellectual concept of Truth and his baptizing means a mental cleansing. The name *Salim* means "peace." "Near Salim" signifies the illumined consciousness of spiritual life and peace in the individual. The water refers to a natural rising in consciousness of the cleansing power of the thought and word of purification and life. The Jew symbolizes an inquiring thought. John candidly explained that he had said before that Jesus was the Christ, the Saviour, and that he, John, must decrease while the Christ must increase. However John declared that he truly believed Jesus to be the Saviour and that all who believed should receive eternal life. But John must decrease, and yet by his own admission those who believe are to have everlasting life.

Metaphysically interpreted, John the Baptist (representing the illumined intellect) decreases on the sense plane in proportion as the intellect is lifted up in Spirit and is in truth swallowed up in spiritual consciousness. The faculty decreases on one plane only to be reborn on a higher one. The illumined intellect wholly co-operates with Spirit, so there is a merging and blending of these powers until the mere intellect ceases to be mere intellect and is swallowed up in Spirit. This is the ideal unfoldment. There are those who are so bound in their own beliefs, who are so set on the letter of the law, that they think intellectuality is the highest unfoldment. They have not yet attained the ability to perceive or receive the things of Spirit. Those in the John the Baptist process of unfoldment willingly cooperate with the Christ every step of the way. The truth is that we are all under the law of infinite expansion, and the development of the race must go forward. Therefore, it is said that "the Son of man must be lifted up."

An example of how the intellect serves may be readily illustrated by the use of the $x$ in algebra. The $x$ stands for the unknown quantity. When the problem is worked out the $x$ is erased. Thus the intellect is the tool of Spirit just as the $x$ is a tool used in the mathematical operation. In the John the Baptist consciousness we obey and conform our thinking to the requirements of the spiritual instead of the natural. Spirit life is something that has enduring qualities. It is superior to the life that goes and comes through death and rebirth.

When the redeemed intellect is fully merged with the Christ light, then the indwelling Spirit of truth is free to perform many so-called miracles. It bridges over difficulties and cements the forces of the soul into one perfect instrument of God for achieving the glory of God. When one reaches this plane spiritual unfoldment goes forward by leaps and bounds.

In order to fulfill the divine law of his being man must realize that he is the Son of God in manifestation, that he came from above and is above all; also that in his evolution he leaves the earthly consciousness and ascends into the spiritual under a law of mind. "He that cometh from above is above all: he that is of the earth is of the earth, and of the earth he speaketh." For he whom God hath sent speaketh the words of God. "The Father loveth the Son, and hath given all things into his hand."

# *John: Chapter 4*

When therefore the Lord knew that the Pharisees
had heard that Jesus was making and baptizing more
disciples than John 2 (although Jesus himself baptized not, but his disciples), 3 he left Judæa, and departed again into Galilee. 4 And he must needs pass
through Samaria. 5 So he cometh to a city of Samaria,
called Sychar, near to the parcel of ground that Jacob
gave to his son Joseph: 6 and Jacob's well was there.
Jesus therefore, being wearied with his journey, sat
thus by the well. It was about the sixth hour.

T HE NAME *Samaria* means "watchtower"; and
Samaria represents that department of the objective consciousness which functions through
the head. The name *Sychar* means "drunken," and
the place symbolizes a confused state of mind. Sychar was located near the parcel of ground that
Jacob gave to his son Joseph; physiologically it corresponds to the forehead, seat of intellectual perception. Here also is Jacob's well—inspiration
through the intellect alone.

Jesus—I AM—has been compassing the whole
man, from within to without, and the I AM "rests"
at the point where the intellectual and the spiritual
meet.

7 There cometh a woman of Samaria to draw
water: Jesus saith unto her, Give me to drink. 8 For
his disciples were gone away into the city to buy
food. 9 The Samaritan woman therefore saith unto
him, How is that thou, being a Jew, asketh drink
of me, who am a Samaritan woman? (For Jews have
no dealings with Samaritans.) 10 Jesus answered and
said unto her, If thou knewest the gift of God, and

who it is that saith to thee, Give me to drink; thou wouldest have asked of him, and he would have given thee living water. 11 The woman saith unto him, Sir, thou hast nothing to draw with, and the well is deep: whence then hast thou that living water? 12 Art thou greater than our Father Jacob, who gave us the well, and drank thereof himself, and his sons, and his cattle? 13 Jesus answered and said unto her, Every one that drinketh of this water shall thirst again: 14 but whosoever drinketh of the water that I shall give him shall never thirst; but the water that I shall give him shall become in him a well of water springing up unto eternal life. 15 The woman saith unto him, Sir, give me this water, that I thirst not, neither come all the way hither to draw. 16 Jesus saith unto her, Go, call thy husband, and come hither. 17 The woman answered and said unto him, I have no husband. Jesus saith unto her, Thou saidst well, I have no husband: 18 for thou hast had five husbands; and he whom thou now hast is not thy husband: this hast thou said truly. 19 The woman saith unto him, Sir, I perceive that thou art a prophet. 20 Our fathers worshipped in this mountain; and ye say, that in Jerusalem is the place where men ought to worship. 21 Jesus saith unto her, Woman, believe me, the hour cometh, when neither in this mountain, nor in Jerusalem, shall ye worship the Father. 22 Ye worship that which ye know not: we worship that which we know; for salvation is from the Jews. 23 But the hour cometh, and now is, when the true worshippers shall worship the Father in spirit and truth: for such doth the Father seek to be his worshippers. 24 God is Spirit: and they that worship him must worship in spirit and truth. 25 The woman saith unto him, I know that Messiah cometh (he that is called Christ): when he is come, he will declare unto us all things. 26 Jesus saith unto her, I that speak unto thee am he.

27 And upon this came his disciples; and they marvelled that he was speaking with a woman; yet no man said, What seekest thou? or, Why speakest thou with her? 28 So the woman left her waterpot, and went away into the city, and saith to the people, 29 Come, see a man, who told me all things that *ever* I did: can this be the Christ? 30 They went out of the city, and were coming to him.

Jesus preached one of His greatest sermons to the woman at the well; she was a Samaritan, a heathen. ("Jews have no dealings with Samaritans.") Her highest concept of God was that of a being who had to be worshiped in some temple in Jerusalem or in a certain mountain. Jesus told her, "God is Spirit: and they that worship him must worship in spirit and truth."

To worship God truly we must know where He is and how to approach Him. If, as many teach, God lives in heaven, and heaven is located somewhere in the skies, we have a consciousness of separation from Him, and our approach to Him is uncertain.

But when we know the truth about God, that He is an omnipresent Spirit manifesting Himself to our mind when we think of Him as one with us in Spirit and responding to our every thought, then we know Him as He is.

This lesson on omnipresence needs constant repeating because we function mentally and physically, the material or manifest predominating. Here we are told that Jesus went from Judea to Galilee. Judea connotes Spirit and Galilee connotes manifestation. Jesus told the woman that salvation came from the

Judeans or spiritual-minded. It is easy to understand God as Spirit and man as His spiritual offspring.

The "well of water springing up into eternal life" is the fount of Christ inspiration within man's consciousness. When the seal of material thought is broken this inner spiritual life flows forth peacefully, majestically, vitalizing and renewing mind and body. In the clear light of Truth we are conscious of life as unchanging, eternal.

The Samaritan woman represents the duality of the soul or subconsciousness. It is not the true source of wisdom, although many searchers after Truth fail to distinguish between its revelations and those of Spirit. In Hindu metaphysics it is known as the human and animal soul.

The Samaritans claimed to be descendants of Jacob, and they used portions of the Hebrew Scriptures, but in the eyes of the Israelites the Samaritans were pretenders, not true followers of Jehovah. Thus spiritually enlightened people see in psychic and spiritistic phenomena and the revelations of that branch of occultism an imitation of Truth, without a true understanding of its relation to Spirit.

But the soul must have Truth, and Christ recognizes the soul as worthy; hence this wonderful lesson of John 4:9-26 given to one auditor. The soul draws its life from both the earthly side of existence (Jacob's well) and the spiritual (the Jew), but is destined to draw from a higher fount, omnipotent Spirit. Jesus asked the woman for a drink, which indicates the universality of the spiritual life, present in the Samaritan woman as well as in Jesus.

"The gift of God" to man is eternal life. The soul informed of this truth asks the Father for the manifestation of this life, and there gushes forth a never-failing stream. But where sense consciousness is dominant the soul is slow to see the realities of ideas, thoughts, and words; the sight is fixed on material ways and means: "Thou hast nothing to draw with . . . whence then hast thou that living water?" This is a fair setting forth of the status of the questioning ones of this day who ask the explanation of spiritual things on a material basis.

The Christ is a discerner of thoughts and reads the history of the soul as an open book. When Jesus displayed this ability to the woman, she at once had faith in Him and accepted Him as a prophet, not because she understood His doctrine, but because He had told her of her past: "Come, see a man, who told me all things that *ever* I did."

In its natural state the soul is attached to localities, forms, and conditions in the world. It believes in the importance of places of worship and in the observance of outward forms. The Mind of Spirit puts all such formalities aside and proclaims the universality of spiritual forces. "God is Spirit." "Neither in this mountain, nor in Jerusalem, shall ye worship the Father." The soul, by falling into forms of worship, fails to get the true understanding, but the Christ-minded know Spirit. They enter into the consciousness of the formless life and substance and they are satisfied.

The Jews represent spiritual understanding, inspiration; the Gentiles represent material understanding. Salvation comes only through spiritual inspiration. This is the inner interpretation of Jesus' words "Salvation is from the Jews."

The "woman of Samaria" is a combination of the intellectual and emotional side of the soul. Jesus met her beside Jacob's well (inspiration through the intellect alone) in the city of Sychar (a confused state of mind). The I AM (Jesus) has power to harmonize the intellect by the power of Spirit. But before the I AM can do this, it must get the intelligent attention of the mixed state of consciousness symbolized by Sychar and the Samaritans. Being a combination of both Hebrew and heathen blood, the Samaritans were a mixed race; the woman at the well recognized the separation that exists between absolute Truth and the mixed thoughts of intellect. Jesus is not afraid of being contaminated by such communion. He is willing to imbibe the inspiration of this realm of mind, and in so doing He comes in touch with its interests.

The Jesus consciousness is appealing to intellectual people to recognize the gift of God, the Spirit of universal love and brotherhood. It invites their thoughts to receive the living inspiration, which may be had for the asking. But man must ask. "Ask, and ye shall receive."

The questioning, analytical attitude taken by the woman at the well represents the tendency of intellect to argue: "I see no visible means whereby you can get the everlasting water of life. Are you greater than all the precedents and antecedents of intellectual inheritance and experience?" These assumptions

of the spiritual-minded that they have a truth higher
than human reason seem to be farfetched and
ephemeral. These are but a few of the many questions and objections of the intellectually wise.

Nevertheless spiritual perception continues to
affirm that it has the inspiration that will never
slacken or prove wanting. The mortal understands so
little that it is constantly asking for more. It is never
satisfied with itself or with the knowledge that it
finds; but whoever drinks of the true spiritual inspiration will never thirst. It will prove a "well of
water springing up unto eternal life."

The outer symbol of worship is adoration, homage; but worship in Spirit and Truth involves absolute union with the character of the object of worship. Therefore in order to fulfill the requirements of
spiritual worship, a right understanding of God and
a development in oneself of His Spirit are necessary.

31 In the mean while the disciples prayed him,
saying, Rabbi, eat. 32 But he said unto them, I have
meat to eat that ye know not. 33 The disciples therefore said one to another, Hath any man brought him
*aught* to eat? 34 Jesus saith unto them, My meat is to
do the will of him that sent me, and to accomplish
this work. 34 Say not ye, There are yet four months,
and *then* cometh the harvest? behold, I say unto you,
Lift up your eyes, and look on the fields, that they
are white already unto harvest, 36 He that reapeth
receiveth wages, and gathereth fruit unto life eternal;
that he that soweth and he that reapeth may rejoice together. 37 For herein is the saying true, One soweth,
and another reapeth. 38 I sent you to reap that where-
on ye have not labored: others have labored, and ye
are entered into their labor.

On the divine side of his being man makes contact with spiritual ideas, which are the source of external substance or food. The natural man (represented by the disciples) thinks that the substance necessary for food must be put through the material process of planting and harvesting, but in Spirit the pure substance is always at hand ready to be appropriated by the inner consciousness. In states of high spiritual realization the desire for material food vanishes. Jesus fasted for forty days and "afterward hungered."

> 39 And from that city many of the Samaritans believed on him because of the word of the woman, who testified, He told me all things that *ever* I did. 40 So when the Samaritans came unto him, they besought him to abide with them: and he abode there two days. 41 And many more believed because of his word; 42 and they said to the woman, Now we believe, not because of thy speaking: for we have heard for ourselves, and know that this is indeed the Saviour of the world.

There are always those at hand who need help, and that is our chance to administer aid. The woman who received help from Jesus at the well fled to the city to tell the people of Him. The result was that many came to Him, and He ministered to them all, proving that salvation is for all alike. "God is no respecter of persons." Salvation comes to everyone who assimilates and appropriates these truths and lets them find expression in and through him. Jesus healed and freed those to whom He ministered, and they believed, not because of what the woman said

but because they themselves witnessed what Jesus
Himself did.

> 43 And after the two days he went forth from
> thence into Galilee. 44 For Jesus himself testified,
> that a prophet hath no honor in his own country.
> 45 So when he came into Galilee, the Galilæans re-
> ceived him, having seen all things that he did in
> Jerusalem at the feast: for they also went unto the
> feast.

Jesus came into Galilee, and the Galileans received Him. Spiritually interpreted, this means that
the indwelling Christ reaches spiritual consumma-
tion, spiritual unity with the original Spirit, in the
measure that it manifests life and functions in Spirit
consciousness. Life activity (Galilee) is omnipresent,
and man needs to apprehend the laws of Spirit, the
laws governing all manifest things and his relation
to all things.

The natural man looks up to what he considers
mysterious and wonderful. He is not impressed by
anything he thinks he knows and understands. Miracles to him are expected to come forth from some
miraculous background. Therefore, Jesus, the carpen-
ter's son, was of too common origin for His native
companions to have any great faith in His claims
of spiritual inspiration. "No man is a hero to his
tailor." Therefore the Master "did not many mighty
works there [in Nazareth] because of their unbelief."

> 46 He came therefore again unto Cana of Gali-
> lee, where he made the water wine. And there was

a certain nobleman, whose son was sick at Capernaum. 47 When he heard that Jesus was come out of Judæa into Galilee, he went unto him, and besought *him* that he would come down, and heal his son; for he was at the point of death. 48 Jesus therefore said unto him, Except ye see signs and wonders, ye will in no wise believe. 49 The nobleman saith unto him, Sir, come down ere my child die. 50 So Jesus saith unto him, Go thy way; thy son liveth. The man believed the word that Jesus spake unto him, and he went his way. 51 And as he was now going down, his servants met him, saying, that his son lived. 52 So he inquired of them the hour when he began to amend. They said therefore unto him, Yesterday at the seventh hour the fever left him. 53 So the father knew that *it was* at that hour in which Jesus said unto him, Thy son liveth: and himself believed, and his whole house. 54 This is again the second sign that Jesus did, having come out of Judæa into Galilee.

It is believed by many professing Christians that the healing of the nobleman's son was a miracle performed only to furnish proof that Jesus came from God. A Bible commentator who is counted very wise in Bible interpretation has said: "Miracles have been wrought only to authenticate the bearers of supernatural revelation, so when a revelation is really being given, the dull minds of men should be compelled to discern, and attend to it by works so evidently due to divine power as to demonstrate that the speaker must bring a message directly from God." Yet Jesus Himself taught that those who believed on Him should do the works that He did and greater works.

The fact is that the healing of the nobleman's son is being duplicated every day of the year by modern followers of Jesus' methods, followers who have numberless absent patients, whom they never see yet whom they heal as effectually as Jesus healed the nobleman's son. Unity has similar cases every day, and the testimonials that we receive bear witness to the efficacy of our healing ministry. The light of Truth is shining more brightly today than ever before. The same faith that healed the nobleman's son will heal all persons who open their minds to it and let go of prejudice and unbelief. This fact is being demonstrated to all who are willing to believe.

Faith on the part of the patient or of someone connected with him is found to be an important factor in absent healing. This nobleman had faith that Jesus could heal his son, and when Jesus uttered the positive truth "Go thy way; thy son liveth," he "believed the word."

Spiritual healing is so marvelous and so far beyond the range of human explanation that it may appear to be supernatural. We cannot explain it clearly, but this we know: When we attain oneness with the invisible force that moves the mind, a new and higher energy sweeps through us; the thought is ablaze, and even our spoken words seem alive. When the word or spiritualized thought is sent to a receptive mind, it is conducted like the oscillations of the wireless telegraph; there is a universal thought ether that carries the message.

When the word goes forth from a spiritual center (represented by Jesus and His apostles) it becomes a continuous life-giver to all who believe in the spiritual as the source of life. Through faith they "tune in" and catch the message from the living word. "The words that I have spoken unto you are spirit, and are life." "Heaven and earth shall pass away: but my words shall not pass away."

# John: Chapter 5

After these things there was a feast of the Jews; and Jesus went up to Jerusalem.

JERUSALEM IS the spiritual center in consciousness. A feast in Jerusalem is a receptive state of mind toward all spiritual good, and the appropriation of that good for future use. Jerusalem means "city of peace." When we get deep down into the silent recesses of our soul we realize a stillness and sweetness beyond expression. There is a great peace there, the "peace of God, which passeth all understanding," and a welling up of an indescribable substance that fills the whole consciousness at the point where the inflow of original substance takes place.

2 Now there is in Jerusalem by the sheep *gate* a pool, which is called in Hebrew Bethesda, having five porches. 3 In these lay a multitude of them that were sick, blind, halt, withered, (waiting for the moving of the water. 4 for an angel of the Lord went down at certain seasons into the pool, and troubled the water whosoever then first after the troubling of the water stepped in was made whole, with whatsoever disease he was holden—margin.) 5 And a certain man was there, who had been thirty and eight years in his infirmity. 6 When Jesus saw him lying, and knew that he had been now a long time *in that case,* he saith unto him, Wouldest thou be made whole? 7 The sick man answered him, Sir, I have no man, when the water is troubled, to put me into the pool: but while I am coming, another steppeth down before me. 8 Jesus saith unto him, Arise, take up thy bed, and walk. 9 And straightway the man was made whole, and took up his bed and walked.

Sheep are the most harmless and innocent of all animals, and they represent the natural life that flows into man's consciousness from Spirit. It is pure, innocent, guileless; and when we open our mind to this realization of Spirit life we open the gate by the sheep market.

Here is a pool called Bethesda (meaning "house of mercy" or "place of receiving and caring for the sick"). There are also five porches or covered colonnades. This "pool" represents the realization in consciousness that our life is being constantly purified, healed, and made new by the activity of mind. Physically this is expressed in the purification and upbuilding of the blood by coming in contact with the oxygen of the air in the lungs. The ebb and flow of the waters of the pool is constant, and when our mind is active all the depleted blood corpuscles are purified and renewed.

This great multitude of "sick folk" (depleted life corpuscles) lies near this pool, under the "five porches" (five senses). The "five-sense" consciousness does not realize the power of the I AM to quicken these inner functions of man's organism; it lets weak, depleted life cells accumulate and burden its system, when a thought of the activity of life would, through the divine law, set them free from their helplessness.

It is not necessary that all the purification and renewing of the depleted corpuscles take place through the lungs when man understands the power of the I AM to declare the word of activity. Jesus, the I AM of Spirit, did not tell the man to go down into the pool and be healed, but said, "Arise, take up thy bed, and walk." Thus we see that the work of the Spirit is not confined to physical activities, although it does not ignore them. If your lung capacity is not equal to the purification of your blood, increase it by declaring the law of active life. Anemic blood may be made vigorous and virile by daily centering the attention in the lungs and affirming them to be spiritual, and under the perpetual inflow of new life and the outflow of old life the lungs will do your will.

Do not be limited by so-called established laws of nature, or by man's mortal thought that if you have reached the age of "thirty-eight" the life current is beginning to wane, that your "sabbath" or day of rest is setting in. It is "lawful" in Spirit to declare the perpetual activity of life anywhere, at any time, and under all circumstances. Divine life takes no cognizance of the laws that the intellect has set up for governing it. Life is ever active. It is constantly present in all its fullness and power, and it has no day of rest or "sabbath."

Now it was the sabbath on that day. 10 So the Jews said unto him that was cured, It is the sabbath, and it is not lawful for thee to take up thy bed. 11 But he answered them, He that made me whole, the same said unto me, Take up thy bed, and walk. 12 They asked him, Who is the man that said unto thee, Take up *thy bed,* and walk? 13 But he that was healed knew not who it was; for Jesus had conveyed himself away, a multitude being in the place. 14 Afterward Jesus findeth him in the temple, and said unto him, Behold, thou art made whole: sin no more, lest a

worse thing befall thee. 15 The man went away,
and told the Jews that it was Jesus who had made
him whole. 16 And for this cause the Jews persecuted Jesus, because he did these things on the sabbath. 17 But Jesus answered them, My Father worketh even until now, and I work. 18 For this cause
therefore the Jews sought the more to kill him, because he not only brake the sabbath, but also called
God his own Father, making himself equal with God.

These particular Jews had no understanding of
the real "sabbath," which is a state of consciousness
attained through meditation and the realization that
the law is fulfilled in both thought and act.

The "sabbath of the Lord" has nothing to do
with any day of the week. God did not name days
and weeks, nor has He darkened His clear concepts
of Truth by the time element.

Therefore, it is during the period of rest known
as the "sabbath" that the demonstrations come forth,
the state of consciousness in which the man that was
sick let go of all false appearances and took up his
bed and walked.

Many times much outer discord is avoided by the
Christ's seemingly withdrawing from the outer until
the quibbling intellect has somewhat spent its fury.
("Jesus had conveyed himself away.") Then the
Christ reappears and reveals to the demonstrating
thought added light: "Sin no more, lest a worse
thing befall thee."

God-Mind is the living power back of all nature,
causing the flowers to bud and to bloom and the
grass to spring up. Jesus explained the outer working of this law in a very few words when He said,

"My Father worketh even until now, and I work."

This divine creative power works continually one day just the same as any other day. Metaphysically we realize that this great creative force is God-Mind in action, and that it can not only create but also re-create. Therefore when Jesus spoke the word for him the sick man through this redeeming agency was instantly made whole. As all sickness is the result of sin, he who was healed was admonished to refrain from again breaking the law lest a worse sickness befall him.

Jesus was introducing into the consciousness of man the new truth that God is indeed the loving Father of all. But the intellectualists (represented by the Pharisees) could not receive it.

"He not only brake the sabbath [from the viewpoint of the Pharisees], but also called God his own Father, making himself equal with God."

Here again the Jews thought it blasphemy even to consider spiritualizing their nature until they knew in deed and in truth that God was their Father and that all that the Father had was theirs.

19 Jesus therefore answered and said unto them, Verily, verily, I say unto you, The Son can do nothing of himself, but what he seeth the Father doing: for what things soever he doeth, these the Son also doeth in like manner. 20 For the Father loveth the Son, and showeth him all things that himself doeth: and greater works than these will he show him, that ye may marvel. 21 For as the Father raiseth the dead and giveth them life, even so the Son also giveth life to whom he will. 22 For neither doth the Father judge any man, but he hath given all judgment unto

the Son; 23 that all may honor the Son, even as they honor the Father. He that honoreth not the Son honoreth not the Father that sent him. 24 Verily, verily, I say unto you, He that heareth my word, and believeth him that sent me, hath eternal life, and cometh not into judgment, but hath passed out of death into life. 25 Verily, verily, I say unto you, The hour cometh, and now is, when the dead shall hear the voice of the Son of God; and they that hear shall live. 26 For as the Father hath life in himself, even so gave he to the Son also to have life in himself: 27 and he gave him authority to execute judgment, because he is a son of man. 28 Marvel not at this: for the hour cometh, in which all that are in the tombs shall hear his voice, 29 and shall come forth; they that have done good, unto the resurrection of life; and they that have done evil, unto the resurrection of judgment.

The Father is the great source of all light and all understanding, and the Son is the idea that expresses the light and the wisdom of God.

The Son is the idea of God-Mind, of man in his perfection. Under divine law man makes manifest what God has in His mind.

The divine idea, the Christ, has been given eternal life and has the power to impart it to the Adam man. In addition to this He has been given judgment: He determines how the life shall be made manifest. The Father of life is a great river in the Garden of Eden, which represents man's innate capacity ready to obtain expression in all wisdom and understanding.

We honor the Christ when we recognize it as having the authority of God. In its life-giving capacity it is equal to God and has the power of God. When that is enthroned in us which possesses spiritual identity we have the realization that we are speaking the word right from the Father. Jesus in this state of unfoldment proclaimed: "The words that I say unto you I speak not from myself: but the Father abiding in me doeth his works."

In this way God is most fully manifest in His "divine idea" or Son, the Christ in man.

What men need above all else in this day is more wisdom, more discretion, in the use of the life they have. More life accompanied by the same old destructive ignorance in using it would but add to their misery. Thus God does not dictate what shall be man's choice with respect to this or any other act. If man discovers the law through which life is made manifest in his consciousness, he may use it blindly and ignorantly if he so elects. But he must also abide by the results of his choosing, and this is where man sets up his wail of sorrow: he does not like to reap his sowing.

Death came into our world through the ignorant use of life, and death can be put out only by a wise use of life. Death is the result of a wrong conception of life and its use. In the beginning of man's experiments with the powers of Being, he had no conception of death. His consciousness was intact and his unfoldment in wisdom was gradual and orderly. But his desire to experiment predominated. Sensation was sweet and enticing; it absorbed so much of his attention that he forgot wisdom—he "hid" from his Lord, and the result was separation from his

Eden, the divine harmony of the law of spiritual unfoldment.

In raising the dead there are then two factors to deal with. The thought of the reality of death and the fear of death have both played destructive roles in the race consciousness, and they must be taken up and dissolved. The total unreality of death must be portrayed to the deluded consciousness. The omnipresence and the omnipotence of life are beyond dispute, and there can be no question that death is a condition set up in human consciousness. God is not dead; He does not recognize or countenance death. Neither does man when freed from its delusion. Jesus said: "Follow me . . . Leave the dead to bury their own dead."

The first step in demonstrating over death is to get the belief entirely out of the mind that it is God-ordained or is of force or effect anywhere in the realm of pure Being.

The next step is to live so harmoniously that the whole consciousness will be not only resurrected from its belief in death but so vivified and energized with the idea of undying life that it cannot be dissolved or separated from its vehicle, the body.

If our thoughts are good they work for good in our life, and if they are bad they are objects of redemption.

> 30 I can of myself do nothing; as I hear, I judge: and my judgment is righteous; because I seek not mine own will, but the will of him that sent me. 31 If I bear witness of myself, my witness is not true. 32 It is another that beareth witness of me; and I know that the witness which he witnesseth of me

is true. 33 Ye have sent unto John, and he hath borne witness unto the truth. 34 But the witness which I receive is not from man: howbeit I say these things, that ye may be saved. 35 He was the lamp that burneth and shineth; and ye were willing to rejoice for a season in his light. 36 But the witness which I have is greater than *that of* John; for the works which the Father hath given me to accomplish, the very works that I do, bear witness of me, that the Father hath sent me. 37 And the Father that sent me, he hath borne witness of me. Ye have neither heard his voice at any time, nor seen his form. 38 And ye have not his word abiding in you: for whom he sent, him ye believe not. 39 Ye search the scriptures, because ye think that in them ye have eternal life; and these are they which bear witness of me; 40 and ye will not come to me, that ye may have life. 41 I receive not glory from men. 42 But I know you, that ye have not the love of God in yourselves. 43 I am come in my Father's name, and ye receive me not: if another shall come in his own name, him ye will receive. 44 How can ye believe, who receive glory one of another, and the glory that *cometh* from the only God ye seek not? 45 Think not that I will accuse you to the Father: there is one that accuseth you, *even* Moses, on whom ye have set your hope. 46 For if ye believed Moses, ye would believe me; for he wrote of me. 47 But if ye believe not his writings, how shall ye believe my words?

The Christ is the perfect God idea, which is ever in touch with its source. The Christ therefore realizes always that it can of itself do nothing, and places all judgment in the law. The laws of God are unchangeable. Man neither makes nor creates anything of permanence; he discerns what God has created and conforms to it in thought and act.

Judgment, when expressed on the mortal plane of consciousness, often is the expression of a critical and backbiting disposition. Man's safety lies in recognizing his need and balancing his judgment faculty with love. Then there will spring forth a new conquering power, which will express itself in righteousness and justice without condemnation.

The substitution of the Scriptures for the living Word of God is undoubtedly one of the reasons why the promise of Jesus to His followers of the ability to do mighty works has not been fulfilled. The Jews of Jesus' time had done this very thing: they had substituted the Book of Moses for the living Word and had so materialized their minds and their religion that they did not know the Messiah when He came. Jesus accused them of this, saying: "Ye search the scriptures, because ye think that in them ye have eternal life; and these are they which bear witness of me; and ye will not come to me, that ye may have life."

The Scriptures alone are not sufficient to impart spiritual understanding. The Pharisees were inveterate students of the Hebrew Scriptures, but Jesus accused them repeatedly of lack of understanding. The Bible is a sealed book to one whose own spiritual understanding has not been quickened by the living Word. "The word is very nigh unto thee, in thy mouth, and in thy heart, that thou mayest do it." Jesus so identified Himself with the living Word that His words became, like it, creative. He submerged His personality in God-Mind until He became the expression of that Mind, the idea clothed in flesh. "And the Word became flesh, and dwelt among us." Then instead of memorizing whole chapters of the Bible let us quicken our mind and our body with the creative word and thereby escape death. "Verily, verily, I say unto you, If a man keep my word, he shall never see death."

The Pharisaical mind thinks that salvation lies in the Scripture itself, when in fact the Scripture simply bears witness of the Saviour. The need is not to concentrate on the letter of the law but to live the Truth and let the divine principles find expression through the soul. Thus man learns to travel the path that leads to light and peace and satisfaction.

There is no necessity of accusing our brother. The law itself works everything out in perfect justice. In fact Moses symbolizes this progressive or "drawing-out" process, which in the individual works from within upward, and in the universe appears as the upward trend of all things.

The idea that the Bible is the living Word of God has diverted the attention of Christians from the one creative Word ever since the original translators dropped the little word "ye" from the sentence (in John 5:39) in which Jesus criticized the Jews for their much study of the Scriptures and thereby made their study a command. Modern translators have corrected this attempt to make Jesus an indorser of the printed word, and it is now made clear that overstudy of the letter may prevent one from making unity with the Word of God manifest, Jesus the Christ.

# John: Chapter 6

After these things Jesus went away to the other side of the sea of Galilee, which is *the sea* of Tiberias. 2 And a great multitude followed him, because they beheld the signs which he did on them that were sick. 3 And Jesus went up into the mountain, and there he sat with his disciples. 4 Now the passover, the feast of the Jews, was at hand. 5 Jesus therefore lifting up his eyes, and seeing that a great multitude cometh unto him, saith unto Philip, Whence are we to buy bread, that these may eat? 6 And this he said to prove him: for he himself knew what he would do. 7 Philip answered him, Two hundred shillings' worth of bread is not sufficient for them, that every one may take a little. 8 One of his disciples, Andrew, Simon Peter's brother, saith unto him, 9 There is a lad here, who hath five barley loaves, and two fishes: but what are these among so many? 10 Jesus said, Make the people sit down. Now there was much grass in the place. So the men sat down, in number about five thousand. 11 Jesus therefore took the loaves; and having given thanks, he distributed to them that were set down; likewise also of the fishes as much as they would. 12 And when they were filled, he saith unto his disciples, Gather up the broken pieces which remain over, that nothing be lost. 13 So they gathered them up, and filled twelve baskets with broken pieces from the five barley loaves, which remained over unto them that had eaten. 14 When therefore the people saw the sign which he did, they said, This is of a truth the prophet that cometh into the world.

WE INCREASE our vitality by blessing and giving thanks in spirit. To bring about this increase efficiently we must understand the anatomy of the soul and mind centers in the body.

It has been found by experience that a person increases his blessings by being grateful for what he has. Gratitude even on the mental plane is a great magnet, and when gratitude is expressed from the spiritual standpoint it is powerfully augmented. The custom of saying grace at the table has its origin in man's attempt to use this power of increase.

A woman who had been left with a large family and no visible means of support related in an experience meeting how wonderfully this law had worked in providing food for her children. In her extremity she had asked the advice of one who understood the law, and she had been told to thank God silently for abundant supply on her table, regardless of appearances. She and her children began doing this, and in a short time the increase of food was so great at times that it astonished them. Her grocer's bill was met promptly, and in most marvelous ways the family was supplied with food. Never after that time did they lack.

In all its work the I AM (Christ) uses the faculties of the mind. The I AM is Spirit, and it cannot move directly on substance or formed states of consciousness. It uses the spiritual faculties as its agents. The name *Philip* means "power," and Jesus appealed to Philip to know how these hungry "thoughts" or people were to be fed. Jesus did this to "prove him." This means that power is still under the limitations of sense. It looks on the visible supply and judges its capacity from that viewpoint. Andrew (strength), brother of Peter (faith), has a slight perception of true supply on the seven-sense plane of consciousness (represented as the lad with five loaves and two fishes). This is a good beginning for the I AM. If you have a consciousness of the capacity that is involved in the natural man's sevenfold nature, you have a good foundation on which to build the twelvefold or spiritual man.

Having quickened your idea of power and strength in universal Spirit, you "sit down" or center your forces within you and begin to bless and give thanks. In divine order you make connection with the universal, vital energy of Being and fill your whole consciousness with vitality. The surplus energy settles back into the various centers as reserve force (the twelve baskets that remained over). Thus you learn to live by "the living bread which came down out of heaven," the very flesh or substance of eternal life.

Jesus and His disciples were on a mountain when this great increase of substance took place, which indicates a high state of consciousness. An eminent British scientist, Sir James Jeans, says that it may be that the gods that determine our fates are our own minds acting on our brain cells and through them on the world about us. Here is stated a profound truth that, accepted and tested, will demonstrate supply to meet every need. Science says that we live in an invisible ether pregnant with the essence of all visible things, that this essence is wrapped up in the atom, and that it awaits an as yet undiscovered law to set it free. Jesus knew the law and through Him we may know it. In World War II science used this power in the destructive atom bomb. Jesus used it constructively in feeding the five thousand.

> 15 Jesus therefore perceiving that they were
> about to come and take him by force, to make him
> king, withdrew again into the mountain himself
> alone.

Spirit always has the power and the ability to handle any situation. Jesus knew His time had not yet come. He had not yet developed the spiritual power necessary to meet the many demands made on Him. The way out was to withdraw from public work for a season. Those who are evolving spiritually know whether or not they are equal to certain demands made on them, and they withdraw to the within for further spiritual realization and power.

> 16 And when evening came, his disciples went
> down unto the sea; 17 and they entered into a boat,
> and were going over the sea unto Capernaum. And
> it was now dark, and Jesus had not yet come to
> them. 18 And the sea was rising by reason of a great
> wind that blew. 19 When therefore they had rowed
> about five and twenty or thirty furlongs, they behold
> Jesus walking on the sea, and drawing nigh unto the
> boat: and they were afraid. 20 But he saith unto
> them, It is I; be not afraid. 21 They were willing
> therefore to receive him into the boat: and straight-
> way the boat was at the land whither they were
> going.

To walk on the sea as Jesus did, without sinking down into the waves, required established faith in the power of Spirit.

We cannot walk on the waves of life in our

own personal strength. If we remember to call on the strength of Christ we are sustained by unlimited power, by the real self.

22 On the morrow the multitude that stood on the other side of the sea saw that there was no other boat there, save one, and that Jesus entered not with his disciples into the boat, but *that* his disciples went away alone 23 (howbeit there came boats from Tiberias nigh unto the place where they ate the bread after the Lord had given thanks): 24 when the multitude therefore saw that Jesus was not there, neither his disciples, they themselves got into the boats, and came to Capernaum, seeking Jesus. 25 And when they found him on the other side of the sea, they said unto him, Rabbi, when camest thou hither? 26 Jesus answered them and said, Verily, verily, I say unto you, Ye seek me, not because ye saw signs, but because ye ate of the loaves, and were filled. 27 Work not for the food which perisheth, but for the food which abideth unto eternal life, which the Son of man shall give unto you: for him the Father, *even* God, hath sealed. 28 They said therefore unto him, What must we do, that we may work the works of God? 29 Jesus answered and said unto them, This is the work of God, that ye believe on him whom he hath sent. 30 They said therefore unto him, What then doest thou for a sign, that we may see, and believe thee? what workest thou? 31 Our fathers ate the manna in the wilderness; as it is written, He gave them bread out of heaven to eat. 32 Jesus therefore said unto them, Verily, verily, I say unto you, It was not Moses that gave you the bread out of heaven; but my Father giveth you the true bread out of heaven. 33 For the bread of God is that which cometh down out of heaven, and giveth life unto the world. 34 They said therefore unto him, Lord, evermore give us this bread. 35 Jesus said

unto them, I am the bread of life: he that cometh to me shall not hunger, and he that believeth on me shall never thirst. 36 But I said unto you, that ye have seen me, and yet believe not. 37 All that which the Father giveth me shall come unto me; and him that cometh to me I will in no wise cast out. 38 For I am come down from heaven, not to do mine own will, but the will of him that sent me. 39 And this is the will of him that sent me, that of all that which he hath given me I should lose nothing, but should raise it up at the last day. 40 For this is the will of my Father, that every one that beholdeth the Son, and believeth on him, should have eternal life; and I will raise him up at the last day.

41 The Jews therefore murmured concerning him, because he said, I am the bread which came down out of heaven. 42 And they said, Is not this Jesus, the son of Joseph, whose father and mother we know? how doth he now say, I am come down out of heaven? 43 Jesus answered and said unto them, Murmur not among yourselves. 44 No man can come to me, except the Father that sent me draw him: and I will raise him up in the last day. 45 It is written in the prophets, And they shall all be taught of God. Every one that hath heard from the Father, and hath learned, cometh unto me. 46 Not that any man hath seen the Father, save he that is from God, he hath seen the Father. 47 Verily, verily, I say unto you, He that believeth hath eternal life. 48 I am the bread of life. 49 Your fathers ate the manna in the wilderness, and they died. 50 This is the bread which cometh down out of heaven, that a man may eat thereof, and not die. 51 I am the living bread which came down out of heaven: if any man eat of this bread, he shall live for ever: yea and the bread which I will give is my flesh, for the life of the world.

52 The Jews therefore strove one with another,

saying, How can this man give us his flesh to eat? 53
Jesus therefore said unto them, Verily, verily, I say unto you, Except ye eat the flesh of the Son of man and
drink his blood, ye have not life in yourselves. 54 He
that eateth my flesh and drinketh my blood hath eternal life; and I will raise him up at the last day. 55 For
my flesh is meat indeed, and my blood is drink indeed. 56 He that eateth my flesh and drinketh my
blood abideth in me, and I in him. 57 As the living
Father sent me, and I live because of the Father; so he
that eateth me, he also shall live because of me. 58
This is the bread which came down out of heaven; not
as the fathers ate, and died; he that eateth this bread
shall live for ever. 59 These things said he in the
synagogue, as he taught in Capernaum.

Here the multitudes (meaning a multitude of
thoughts) are really seeking comfort and consolation
("they themselves got into the boats and came to
Capernaum, seeking Jesus"). They had entered into that inner conviction of the abiding compassion
and restoring power of God.

In the universal Mind principle, which Jesus
called "the Father," there is a substance that also includes the mother or seed of all visible substance. It
is the only real substance because it is unchangeable,
while the visible substance is in constant transition.

The origin or source of all substance is the idea
of substance. It is purely spiritual and can be ap-
prehended only by the mind. It is never visible to
the eye, nor can it be sensed by man through any of
the bodily faculties. Bible authorities say that the Almighty God in Genesis should have been translated

El Shaddai, "the breasted one." Thus God is found to include both the male and the female principle.

When the mind has centered its attention on this idea of substance long enough and strongly enough, it generates the consciousness of substance, and through the powers of the various faculties of the mind in right relation it can form visible substance. Jesus in this way brought into visibility the loaves and fishes to feed the five thousand.

But this faculty of dealing with ideas is open to all men and women. It is not given to privileged persons and withheld from all others.

Jesus knew this, and He also knew that every man must center his attention on this spiritual substance and bring forth its fruits, just as He did. But those whose attention has long been centered in things visible are slow to appreciate this fact.

Jesus fed the multitude in an easy way, and they followed Him over the sea in boats apparently in order to get more food; at least that is the motive Jesus attributed to them.

Then He tells them plainly that they must not labor for the food that perishes but for the food that "abideth unto eternal life."

When they asked how they should do these "works of God" or so-called miracles, He said, "Believe on him whom he hath sent." One translation says, "Believe in him." Man is to believe in the spiritual presence of the living God even as one "sent"; that is, entered into the consciousness.

All shall attain who believe or have faith in the spiritual source of life. Whoever comes to this Christ realm in the heavens all about us will be moved by its will, which is the will of the Father. There will be no loss, no failure in this realm, and whoever enters into the Mind of Spirit will have poured out to him its life essence and be wholly raised up from material conditions when arriving at the "last day" (the last degree of understanding).

Moses caused manna to fall from heaven to feed the Children of Israel. The body of Christ is a spiritual substance that we incorporate into consciousness through faith out of the heavens of mind. That the food we eat has a spiritual source is proved by those who fast in spiritual faith much longer and easier than those who are forced to starve.

60 Many therefore of his disciples, when they heard *this,* said, This is a hard saying; who can hear it? 61 But Jesus knowing in himself that his disciples murmured at this, said unto them, Doth this cause you to stumble? 62 *What* then if ye should behold the Son of man ascending where he was before? 63 It is the spirit that giveth life; the flesh profiteth nothing: the words that I have spoken unto you are spirit, and are life. 64 But there are some of you that believe not. For Jesus knew from the beginning who they were that believed not, and who it was that should betray him. 65 And he said, For this cause have I said unto you, that no man can come unto me, except it be given unto him of the Father.

66 Upon this many of his disciples went back, and walked no more with him. 67 Jesus said therefore unto the twelve, Would ye also go away? 68 Simon Peter answered him, Lord, to whom shall we go? thou hast the words of eternal life. 69 And we have believed and know that thou art the Holy One of God. 70 Jesus answered them, Did not I

choose you the twelve, and one of you is a devil?
71 Now he spake of Judas, *the son* of Simon Iscariot,
for he it was that should betray him, *being* one of the
twelve.

Jesus said, "It is the spirit that giveth life; the
flesh profiteth nothing: the words that I have spoken
unto you are spirit, and are life." Being, the original
fount, is an impersonal principle; but in its work of
creation it puts forth an idea that contains all ideas:
the Logos, Word, Christ, the Son of God, or spiritual
man. This spiritual man or Christ or Word of God
is the true inner self of every individual. Man therefore contains within himself the capacities of Being,
and through his words uses the creative principle in
forming his environment, good or bad. So we make
our own heaven or hell.

The ideas that make words constructive are those
of life, love, wisdom, substance, power, strength, and
all other ideas that express divine attributes. Words
carrying the life idea produce a vitalizing and life-
giving effect. Words that express divine love are harmonizing and unifying in their effect.

Words are made active in the body through their
receptivity by the mind and are carried into the
body through the subconsciousness by one's thought.
Constructive words that renew the body are made a
part of the body consciousness by prayer and meditation. These are the words that are Spirit and give
life.

Many people start out to walk in the light of
Spirit, to unfold Truth, but they become entangled
in their own misgivings and disbelief and therefore

return to their old limited way of life.

After these events Jesus went to Galilee (the "whirl of life"), for He did not walk in Judea (praise) because the Jews sought to kill him. The Jews (the Pharisaical Jews in this instance) believed in the letter of the law rather than the spirit.

# John: Chapter 7

And after these things Jesus walked in Galilee:
for he would not walk in Judæa, because the Jews
sought to kill him. 2 Now the feast of the Jews, the
feast of tabernacles, was at hand. His brethren therefore said unto him, Depart hence, and go into Judæa,
that thy disciples also may behold thy works which
thou doest. 4 For no man doeth anything in secret,
and himself seeketh to be known openly. If thou
doest these things, manifest thyself to the world. 5
For even his brethren did not believe on him. 6 Jesus
therefore saith unto them, My time is not yet come;
but your time is always ready. 7 The world cannot
hate you; but me it hateth, because I testify of it,
that its works are evil. 8 Go ye up unto the feast: I
go not up unto this feast; because my time is not yet
fulfilled. 9 And having said these things unto them,
he abode *still* in Galilee.

10 But when his brethren were gone up unto the
feast, then went he also up, not publicly, but as it
were in secret. 11 The Jews therefore sought him at
the feast, and said, Where is he? 12 And there was
much murmuring among the multitudes concerning
him: some said, He is a good man; others said, Not
so, but he leadeth the multitude astray. 13 Yet no
man spake openly of him for fear of the Jews.

JESUS WAS DEVELOPING His spiritual nature,
which is under spiritual law. The Pharisaical
Jews followed the letter of the law, which resists and seeks the destruction of the Christ. The
Christ usually moves in secret. It does its spiritual
work quietly instead of showing off. Some of the
multitude thought Jesus was a good man; others
thought He had led the people astray. This represents the quibbling of the lesser mind.

14 But when it was now the midst of the feast
Jesus went up into the temple, and taught. 15 The
Jews therefore marvelled, saying, How knowest this
man letters, having never learned? 16 Jesus therefore answered them, and said, My teaching is not
mine, but his that sent me. 17 If any man willeth to
do his will, he shall know of the teaching, whether
it is of God, or *whether* I speak from myself. 18 He
that speaketh from himself seeketh his own glory:
but he that seeketh the glory of him that sent him,
the same is true, and no unrighteousness is in him.
19 Did not Moses give you the law, and *yet* none of
you doeth the law? Why seek ye to kill me? 20 The
multitude answered, Thou hast a demon: who seeketh to kill thee? 21 Jesus answered and said unto
them, I did one work, and ye all marvel because
thereof. 22 Moses hath given you circumcision (not
that it is of Moses, but of the fathers); and on the
sabbath ye circumcise a man. 23 If a man receiveth
circumcision on the sabbath, that the law of Moses
may not be broken; are ye wroth with me, because I
made a man every whit whole on the sabbath? 24
Judge not according to appearance, but judge righteous judgment.

25 Some therefore of them of Jerusalem said,
Is not this he whom they seek to kill? 26 And
lo, he speaketh openly, and they say nothing unto
him. Can it be that the rulers indeed know that
this is the Christ? 27 Howbeit we know this man
whence he is: but when the Christ cometh, no one
knoweth whence he is. 28 Jesus therefore cried in
the temple, teaching and saying, Ye both know me,
and know whence I am; and I am not come to myself, but he that sent me is true, whom ye know
not. 29 I know him; because I am from him, and he
sent me. 30 They sought therefore to take him: and
no man laid his hand on him, because his hour was
not yet come. 31 But of the multitude many believed

on him; and they said, When the Christ shall come, will he do more signs than those which this man hath done? 32 The Pharisees heard the multitude murmuring these things concerning him; and the chief priests and the Pharisees sent officers to take him. 33 Jesus therefore said, Yet a little while am I with you, and I go unto him that sent me. 34 Ye shall seek me, and shall not find me: and where I am, ye cannot come. 35 The Jews therefore said among themselves, Whither will this man go that we shall not find him? will he go unto the Dispersion among the Greeks, and teach the Greeks? 36 What is this word that he said, Ye shall seek me, and shall not find me; and where I am, ye cannot come?

Jesus' disciples wanted Him to go up to Jerusalem for one reason: to prove that He was the Christ, but He realized that He had not yet attained the necessary power. After they had departed He got more spiritual consciousness and was moved to go under the protection of Spirit, and in this state of mind the Jews could not lay their hands on Him or injure Him in any way. Jesus, like all persons who are growing spiritually, felt the power within Him to be much stronger than He could manifest without. He wanted to prove to His friends that He was the Christ but doubted His ability.

He was not speaking from Himself for His own glory, but He was seeking the glory of Him that sent Him.

The all-knowing Christ Mind can easily handle the Pharisaical mind that is following the letter of the law. The intellectual mind cannot understand the claim of the spiritual that it can go where it cannot be found by those present. The mind that functions in matter cannot comprehend a state in which matter can pass through matter.

> 37 Now on the last day, the great *day* of the feast, Jesus stood and cried, saying, If any man thirst, let him come unto me and drink. 38 He that believeth on me, as the scripture hath said, from within him shall flow rivers of living water. 39 But this spake he of the Spirit, which they that believed on him were to receive: for the Spirit was not yet *given;* because Jesus was not yet glorified.

Jesus realized that man's real thirst is for Spirit and that this thirst can only be quenched through an outpouring of the Holy Spirit within the soul, which thrills one with new life and energy and vitality.

If we have understanding faith we know that there is no cessation of life and that we have only to open our consciousness more and more to the Spirit of life in order to realize that from within flow rivers of living water.

The Holy Spirit was in evidence before the time of Jesus, but He gave a new impetus to this indwelling helper and promised that the holy Comforter would be with us throughout all time.

> 40 *Some* of the multitude therefore, when they heard these words, said, This is of a truth the prophet. 41 Others said, This is the Christ. But some said, What, doth the Christ come out of Galilee? 42 Hath not the scripture said that the Christ cometh of the seed of David, and from Bethlehem, the village where David was? 43 So there arose a division in

the multitude because of him. 44 And some of them
would have taken him; but no man laid hands on
him.

When one is in a mixed state of consciousness
there is always dissension and questioning. However when one is born anew into the Christ consciousness all things are made clear.
    "For all shall know me,
    From the least to the greatest of them."

45 The officers therefore came to the chief priests
and Pharisees; and they said unto them, Why did
ye not bring him? 46 The officers answered, Never
man so spake. 47 The Pharisees therefore answered
them, Are ye also led astray? 48 Hath any of the
rulers believed on him, or of the Pharisees? 49 But
this multitude that knoweth not the law are accursed.
50 Nicodemus saith unto them (he that came to
him before, being one of them), 51 Doth our law
judge a man, except it first hear from himself and
know what he doeth. 52 They answered and said
unto him, Art thou also of Galilee? Search, and see
that out of Galilee ariseth no prophet.

The "chief priests" of the Pharisaical consciousness are the highest thoughts in authority in the
Pharisaical hierarchy. The "officers" are thoughts
that execute the law. However, when it reaches a
certain state of unfoldment even the Pharisaical
mind, which believes in the strict letter of the law,
is open to conviction if it can entertain a higher
truth safely. This is proved by Nicodemus' spiritual
conversion. The Pharisaical side of man's mind in
its faithful adherence to religious forms eventually

becomes aware of the presence of divine power. This truth was in evidence when the officers replied, "Never man so spake," revealing that the higher light of the Christ had found entrance into their consciousness.

# John: Chapter 8

53 [And they went every man unto his own house: 1 but Jesus went unto the mount of Olives. 2 And early in the morning he came again into the temple, and all the people came unto him; and he sat down, and taught them. 3 And the scribes and the Pharisees bring a woman taken in adultery; and having set her in the midst, 4 they say unto him, Teacher, this woman hath been taken in adultery, in the very act. 5 Now in the law Moses commanded us to stone such: what then sayest thou of her? 6 And this they said, trying him, that they might have *whereof* to accuse him. But Jesus stooped down, and with his finger wrote on the ground. 7 But when they continued asking him, he lifted up himself, and said unto them, He that is without sin among you, let him first cast a stone at her. 8 And he again stooped down, and with his finger wrote on the ground. 9 And they, when they heard it, went out one by one, beginning from the eldest, *even* unto the last: and Jesus was left alone, and the woman, where she was, in the midst. 10 And Jesus lifted up himself, and said unto her, Woman, where are they? did no man condemn thee? 11 And she said, No man, Lord. And Jesus said, Neither do I condemn thee: go thy way; from henceforth sin no more.]

JESUS' GOING UP into the Mount of Olives means the soul's ascending to the state of consciousness where absolute Truth is manifest and from this high vantage point teaching a lesson in brotherly love to the intellectual faculties. Sometimes the intellectual faculties imagine they are in supreme authority, as in this case, where the woman caught in adultery is presented as an example. "Now, spiritual man, what are you going to do about that?

Under the law, we are told, we must stone her." Jesus, here symbolizing the indwelling Christ, writes on the ground and says, "He that is without sin among you, let him first cast a stone at her." The intellectual faculties, thus trapped in their own conceit, slink away.

The Christ questions this adulterous state of consciousness: "Woman, where are they? did no man condemn thee?" The reply is "No man, Lord." The final injunction is "Neither do I condemn thee: go thy way; from henceforward sin no more." Thus the overcoming power of the Christ Mind is doing its perfect work.

12 Again therefore Jesus spake unto them, saying, I am the light of the world: he that followeth me shall not walk in the darkness, but shall have the light of life. 13 The Pharisees therefore said unto him, Thou bearest witness of thyself; thy witness is not true. 14 Jesus answered and said unto them, Even if I bear witness of myself, my witness is true; for I know whence I came, and whither I go; but ye know not whence I come, or whither I go. 15 Ye judge after the flesh; I judge no man. 16 Yet and if I judge, my judgment is true; for I am not alone, but I and the Father that sent me. 17 Yea and in your law it is written, that the witness of two men is true. 18 I am he that beareth witness of myself, and the Father that sent me beareth witness of me. 19 They said therefore unto him, Where is thy Father? Jesus answered, Ye know neither me, nor my Father: if ye knew me, ye would know my Father also. 20 These words spake he in the treasury, as he taught in the temple: and no man took him; because his hour was not yet come.

The Christ within is always declaring, "I am the light of the world: he that followeth me shall not walk in the darkness, but shall have the light of life." The first lesson in spiritual development to be learned is that everyone has within him the light of divine understanding. Those who do not recognize that they have this inner light are thinking intellectually instead of spiritually. The Christ light comes forth from God and under all circumstances is aware of its source. It places all judgment in the Father, knowing that its light is from that source alone. The intellectual man has no conception of this truth but depends more on man-made judgment.

Jesus (symbolizing the Christ) was working in the substance consciousness and under the light of Spirit and was master of the situation. Therefore no man took Him, because His hour was not yet come. He put all protection under God, who was ever-present as His witness and defense.

21 He said therefore again unto them, I go away, and ye shall seek me, and shall die in your sin: whither I go, ye cannot come. 22 The Jews therefore said, Will he kill himself, that he saith, Whither I go, ye cannot come? 23 And he said unto them, Ye are from beneath; I am from above: ye are of this world; I am not of this world. 24 I said therefore unto you, that ye shall die in your sins: for except ye believe that I am *he,* ye shall die in your sins. 25 They said therefore unto him, Who art thou? Jesus said unto them, Even that which I have also spoken unto you from the beginning. 26 I have many things to speak and to judge concerning you: howbeit he that sent me is true; and the things which I heard from him, these speak I unto the world. 27 They perceived not that he

spake to them of the Father. 28 Jesus therefore said,
When ye have lifted up the Son of man, then shall ye
know that I am *he,* and *that* I do nothing of myself,
but as the Father taught me, I speak these things. 29
And he that sent me is with me; he hath not left me
alone; for I do always the things that are pleasing to
him. 30 As he spake these things, many believed on
him.

Jesus, symbolizing the I AM, the Christ, again is
proclaiming Truth from the absolute standpoint.
As He persists the light of Christ eventually does
filter into consciousness. Through self-righteous adherence to outer forms man resists his true unfoldment or evolution. The egotistical personality as-
sumes that its world of phenomena is real and that
all talk about disappearing into spirit is illusion.
Sanctimoniousness develops from the belief that intellect can be spiritually sanctified. The spiritual
mind (the I AM) is the Saviour and is working to
come into evidence. It is working to redeem the self-
righteous, Pharisaical, intellectual man. When this
man has been lifted up, "then shall ye know that I
am *he,* and *that* I do nothing of myself, but as the
Father taught me. I speak these things."

31 Jesus therefore said to those Jews that had
believed him, If ye abide in my word, *then* are ye truly
my disciples; 32 and ye shall know the truth, and the
truth shall make you free. 33 They answered unto him,
We are Abraham's seed, and have never yet been in
bondage to any man: how sayest thou, Ye shall be
made free? 34 Jesus answered them, Verily, verily, I
say unto you, Every one that committeth sin is the
bondservant of sin. 35 And the bondservant abideth
not in the house for ever: the son abideth for ever.

36 If therefore the Son shall make you free, ye shall
be free indeed.

An understanding of Truth comes only to those
who abide faithfully in the teachings of Jesus. They
alone are free who persist in holding to the true
view of life, regardless of preaccepted theories, and
who obey only the voice of the higher self, which
holds them to an unswerving performance of the
right, both mental and outer, instead of following
the voice of their own desires.

The subject of freedom is inexhaustible. The
quest of freedom is endless and is unfulfilled save
in the Christ consciousness. The Jews did not understand the teachings of Jesus on this subject. As the
chosen people, they were in bondage to racial pride,
and their intemperance in this regard was difficult
to uproot.

The "house" is man's body. No one who allows
intemperate desires to rule his life and to gain expression through his thought and conduct can hope
to remain long in the body or to experience in it any
measure of true satisfaction. Only the "Son," the
self-forgetting, loving, helpful concentration of all
the powers on the gaining of a higher understanding of the forces that control mankind, can bring
full and complete freedom. Once this power of concentration is gained and practiced, perfect freedom
is indeed assured. But concentration does not spring,
perfect and full-fledged, from beneath the fleeting
wing of the random resolve; it requires the faithful
giving of oneself to the practice of the presence

of God. "Abideth" entails a continuing in the Christ state of mind and heart.

Jesus in effect said, "If you live in the spirit of My teachings, you will become truly My disciples, and you will be freed from all your limitations through the understanding of Truth that comes to you as the result of your steadfastness."

> 37 I know that ye are Abraham's seed: yet ye seek to kill me, because my word hath not free course in you. 38 I speak the things which I have seen with *my* Father: and ye also do the things which ye heard from *your* father. 39 They answered and said unto him, Our father is Abraham. Jesus saith unto them, If ye were Abraham's children, ye would do the works of Abraham. 40 But now ye seek to kill me, a man that hath told you the truth, which I heard from God: this did not Abraham. 41 Ye do the works of your father. They said unto him, We were not born of fornication; we have one Father, *even* God.

Those who think of themselves as descended from human ancestors are in bondage to all the limitations of those ancestors, regardless of their claims to the contrary. It is a falling short of the full stature of man to regard himself as descended from the human family. This is a sin that keeps the majority of men in bondage to sense consciousness. The Jews were proud of their ancestors, Abraham, Isaac, and Jacob, who did things that in our day would make them candidates for the penitentiary. Polygamy might be mentioned as an example.

The worship of ancestors is observed in our own day by those who eagerly search the records of royalty for a family coat of arms or trace their ancestry back to William the Conqueror. The one and only way to get free of this burden of race heredity is to proclaim your divine sonship. If you believe that God is your Father, acknowledge Him, and He will acknowledge you.

A short definition of sin is ignorance. If you knew your spiritual origin and all the purity and power that it includes, you would not be subject to the race tendencies that sway the mind of the flesh. This is the freedom of the Son of God; the shackles of false thoughts are loosed, and there is the open light of heaven instead of the darkness of sense consciousness.

It seems incredible that men should seek to destroy and kill out of their thoughts this superconscious mind, but such is the self-sufficiency of ignorance identified with human lineage. Mortality has failed generation after generation, yet men cling to it as the *summum bonum* of existence, and antagonize the Spirit.

42 Jesus said unto them, If God were your Father, ye would love me: for I came forth and am come from God; for neither have I come of myself, but he sent me. 43 Why do ye not understand my speech? *Even* because ye cannot hear my word. 44 Ye are of *your* father the devil, and the lusts of your father it is your will to do. He was a murderer from the beginning, and standeth not in the truth, because there is no truth in him. When he speaketh a lie, he speaketh of his own: for he is a liar, and the father thereof. 45 But because I say the truth, ye believe me not. 46 Which of you convicteth me of sin? If I say

truth, why do ye not believe me? 47 He that is of
God heareth the words of God: for this cause ye
hear *them* not, because ye are not of God. 48 The
Jews answered and said unto him, Say we not well
that thou art a Samaritan, and hast a demon? 49
Jesus answered, I have not a demon; but I honor my
Father, and ye dishonor me. 50 But I seek not mine
own glory: there is one that seeketh and judgeth.

It is hard for the intellect to realize the spiritual
"I AM THAT I AM." It always argues back and
forth, endeavoring to prove that the intellect itself
is the highest authority.

Jesus condemned the sins of the intellect, of
which self-righteousness is the greatest, as worse
than moral sins. Compare this scathing arraignment
of the arrogant Jews with the ready forgiveness for
the adulteress. The pompous ecclesiastical dignitary
is much harder to reach with Truth than the repent-
ant moral sinner.

Any thought that does not have its origin in the
one divine source is a liar and the father of all lies.

51 Verily, verily, I say unto you. If a man keep
my word, he shall never see death. 52 The Jews said
unto him, Now we know that thou hast a demon.
Abraham died, and the prophets; and thou sayest,
If a man keep my word, he shall never taste of
death. 53 Art thou greater than our father Abraham,
who died? and the prophets died: whom makest thou
thyself? 54 Jesus answered, If I glorify myself, my
glory is nothing: it is my Father that glorifieth me;
of whom ye say, that he is your God; 55 and ye have
not known him: but I know him; and if I should
say, I know him not, I shall be like unto you, a liar:

but I know him, and keep his word. 56 Your father Abraham rejoiced to see my day; and he saw it, and was glad. 57 The Jews therefore said unto him, Thou art not yet fifty years old, and hast thou seen Abraham? 58 Jesus said unto them, Verily, verily, I say unto you, Before Abraham was born, I am. 59 They took up stones therefore to cast at him: but Jesus hid himself, and went out of the temple.

"Verily, verily, I say unto you, If a man keep my word, he shall never see death. The Jews said unto him, Now we know that thou hast a demon. Abraham died, and the prophets; and thou sayest, If a man keep my word, he shall never taste of death."

If the would-be overcomer will diligently meditate on these words, the light of Truth will gradually break in. Then he will know that the Christ, the I AM THAT I AM, was before Abraham and also that the old "church father" Abraham was spiritually quickened to the degree that he was constantly seeking the light. "Your father Abraham rejoiced to see my day; and he saw it, and was glad."

It was the Christ in Jesus who exclaimed, "Before Abraham was born, I am." Christ, the spiritual man, spoke often through Jesus, the natural man. We know that Christ, the spiritual man, could not have experienced death, burial, and resurrection. The experiences were possible only to the mortal man, who was passing from the natural to the spiritual plane of consciousness.

The word of God is the word that conveys to the world the ideas of the Most High. It is not the Most High in His wholeness, but it carries with it the power behind the throne, because "the three agree in one," the Father (principle), the Son (the ideal), and the Holy Ghost, (the formative word).

Jesus said, "If a man keep my word, he shall never see death." The "word" here referred to is not comprehended by the spoken or written word of Jesus but rather the original creative Word of God, the Logos. This is the Logos or God Word that the Gospel of John states "became flesh, and dwelt among us (and we beheld his glory, glory as of the only begotten from the Father)." According to the Bible, the words of Jesus were more powerful than those of any other man who ever lived. He infused the divine-life idea into His words until they made direct union with the creative Word of the Father.

When man in faith makes this intimate connection between his mind and the Father's, he enters into what may be termed the "river of life," and he has ability to take others with him into the waters that cleanse, purify, and vitalize so perfectly that death is swallowed up in life and man lives right on without the tragedy of death. Such a man was, and is, Jesus the Christ, and the promise is that all who incorporate in mind and body the living creative Word, as He did, will with Him escape death. This promise of the overcoming power of the Word has been interpreted to mean death of the soul after physical death, but there is no foundation for this assumption. Jesus overcame death of the body. His followers are expected to do the same.

# *John: Chapter 9*

And as he passed by, he saw a man blind from his birth. 2 And his disciples asked him, saying, Rabbi, who sinned, this man, or his parents, that he should be born blind? 3 Jesus answered, Neither did this man sin, nor his parents: but that the works of God should be made manifest in him. 4 We must work the works of him that sent me, while it is day: the night cometh, when no man can work. 5 When I am in the world, I am the light of the world. 6 When he had thus spoken, he spat on the ground, and made clay of the spittle, and anointed his eyes with the clay, 7 and said unto him, Go, wash in the pool of Siloam (which is by interpretation, Sent). He went away therefore, and washed, and came seeing. 8 The neighbors therefore, and they that saw him aforetime, that he was a beggar, said, Is not this he that sat and begged? 9 Others said, It is he: others said, No, but he is like him. He said, I am *he.* 10 They said therefore unto him, How then were thine eyes opened? 11 He answered, The man that is called Jesus made clay, and anointed mine eyes, and said unto me, Go to Siloam, and wash: so I went away and washed, and I received sight. 12 And they said unto him, Where is he? He saith, I know not.

13 They bring to the Pharisees him that aforetime was blind. 14 Now it was the sabbath on the day when Jesus made the clay, and opened his eyes. 15 Again therefore the Pharisees also asked him how he received his sight. And he said unto them, He put clay upon mine eyes, and I washed, and I see. 16 Some therefore of the Pharisees said, This man is not from God, because he keepeth not the sabbath. But others said, How can a man that is a sinner do such signs? And there was a division among them. 17 They say therefore unto the blind man again, What sayest thou of him, in that he opened thine eyes? And he said, He is a prophet. 18 The

Jews therefore did not believe concerning him, that he had been blind, and had received his sight, until they called the parents of him that had received his sight, 19 and asked them, saying, Is this your son, who ye say was born blind? How then doth he now see? 20 His parents answered and said, We know that this is our son, and that he was born blind: 21 but how he now seeth, we know not; or who opened his eyes, we know not: ask him; he is of age; he shall speak for himself. 22 These things said his parents, because they feared the Jews: for the Jews had agreed already, that if any man should confess him *to be* Christ, he should be put out of the synagogue. 23 Therefore said his parents, He is of age; ask him. 24 So they called a second time the man that was blind, and said unto him, Give glory to God: we know that this man is a sinner. 25 He therefore answered, Whether he is a sinner, I know not: one thing I know, that, whereas I was blind, now I see. 26 They said therefore unto him, What did he to thee? how opened he thine eyes? 27 He answered them, I told you even now, and ye did not hear; wherefore would ye hear it again? would ye also become his disciples? 28 And they reviled him, and said, Thou art his disciple; but we are disciples of Moses. 29 We know that God hath spoken unto Moses: but as for this man, we know not whence he is. 30 The man answered and said unto them, Why, herein is the marvel, that ye know not whence he is, and *yet* he opened mine eyes. 31 We know that God heareth not sinners: but if any man be a worshipper of God, and do his will, him he heareth. 32 Since the world began it was never heard that any one opened the eyes of a man born blind. 33 If this man were not from God, he could do nothing. 34 They answered and said unto him, Thou wast altogether born in sins, and dost thou teach us? And they cast him out.

35 Jesus heard that they had cast him out; and
finding him, he said, Dost thou believe on the Son
of God? 36 He answered and said, And who is he,
Lord, that I may believe on him? 37 Jesus said unto
him, Thou hast both seen him, and he it is that
speaketh with thee. 38 And he said, Lord, I believe.
And he worshipped him. 39 And Jesus said, For
judgment came I into this world, that they that see
not may see; and that they that see may become blind.
40 Those of the Pharisees who were with him heard
these things, and said unto him, Are we also blind?
41 Jesus said unto them. If ye were blind, ye would
have no sin: but now ye say, We see: your sin re-
maineth.

THERE ARE SINS of omission and sins of commission. This text illustrates a sin of omission.
The man born blind had not sinned, neither
had his parents sinned.

In this whole chapter the Christ is declaring, "I
am the light of the world." When our blind, stum-
bling thoughts awaken to the reality of the Christ,
darkness falls away and we see clearly.

The inquiry "Who sinned, this man, or his parents, that he should be born blind?" indicates a pre-
vious incarnation of the man in the fleshly body,
in which he might have sinned. Belief in successive
incarnations of man was accepted by all the scrip-
tural writers who were spiritually wise. The tents
and tabernacles in which the Children of Israel lived
in the wilderness are symbols of the fleshly body that
men put on and off, again and again. Solomon's
Temple is a symbol of the regenerated body of man;
when man attains this body he will cease to die and

reincarnate. In order to build this indestructible body we must make manifest in ourselves the works of God. The Pharisees were very strict in their observance of the external ritual but had no knowledge of the inner spiritual law that expressed its perfection in health of body.

The sin of omission is even greater than the sin of commission. There is some hope for the one who is an active sinner; but what can we expect of one who makes no effort to do anything for himself, who simply drifts with the tide, or looks to others to do all things? Before he was healed, the blind man was a sinner of omission. He was a blind beggar, a person who had no perception of his own capacity, or no confidence in his power to rise superior to conditions in the material realm. When man fails to apprehend his mission and to do the work of bringing forth the good that is allotted to him, he remains in darkness. His blindness is that sin of omission which is present in every man who does not realize his place in the Godhead. If a man fails to do that which he is told from within is the right thing to do, he is sinning, and he will remain in darkness to just the degree that he sins.

The works of God that we are to make manifest are the perfect ideas of a perfect-man idea in Divine Mind. "Ye therefore shall be perfect, as your heavenly Father is perfect." We are to bring forth in ourselves the perfection of Being. If through neglect, laziness, or belief in inability we fail to do this, we fall under the judgment of the constantly operating law of life, which is inwardly urging us and in all the

visible and invisible forms of nature is commanding:
"Go forward."

The world is full of people who are in this beg-
garly blind state. They sit by the wayside and wait
for the workers to give them pennies and crusts,
when they themselves might be the producers of
their own good. The remedy for their situation is
for them to deny material darkness, ignorance, and
inability in themselves. By putting the clay upon
the blind man's eyes Jesus illustrated how man makes
opaque his understanding by affirming the power of
material conditions to hamper and impede his spiritual and material growth. The washing away of this
clay by the man himself shows that by our own
volition and our own efforts we must deny away these
seeming mountains of environing conditions.

The starting point of man's reformation is in the
mind. He must begin to handle situations mentally
at first; as he proceeds to do away with thought limitations, surrounding conditions will gradually
change, and he will find himself "seeing" as a result of his efforts to do the will of the one supreme
Mind.

When we begin to deny away the limitations of
old material race thoughts and to affirm illumination
from the Christ within us, we are sure to arouse the
"Jews" and the "Pharisees" in our mental realm.
They are our tendencies to cling to the letter of the
word, to the forms of religion, and to deny the
power of Spirit actually to illumine our mind and
transform our entire being. If after we are awakened
we are bold in the declaration of Truth, as this man

was when he was healed, we may experience much opposition from our old formal religious ideas. If we listen to them all, we may feel as though we were no longer in spiritual favor. But we need not fear; we shall become conscious of the Christ again, and He will reveal Himself to us. Then we shall worship Him truly.

# John: Chapter 10

Verily, verily, I say unto you, He that entereth
not by the door into the fold of the sheep, but
climbeth up some other way, the same is a thief and
a robber. 2 But he that entereth in by the door is the
shepherd of the sheep. 3 To him the porter openeth;
and the sheep hear his voice: and he calleth his own
sheep by name, and leadeth them out. 4 When he
hath put forth all his own, he goeth before them,
and the sheep follow him: for they know his voice.
5 And a stranger will they not follow, but will flee
from him: for they know not the voice of strangers.
6 This parable spake Jesus unto them: but they understood not what things they were which he spake
unto them.

THE DOOR OF YOUR mind is your open-minded-
ness. "I am the door of the sheep." "Sheep"
are your thoughts. "A thief and a robber" is
mortal thought. The "porter" is the will. The "good
shepherd" is the spiritual I AM.

All forces that come into your consciousness in
any other way than through your own I AM are
thieves and robbers. No man can be saved from
the limitations and mistakes of ignorance except
through his own volition.

There is a widespread belief that we can turn
over to those who have better understanding the
straightening out of our tangled thoughts. Such
help may be extended temporarily, but it always
proves "a thief and a robber" in the end. The true
healer is always the teacher and instructs his patients how to open the door to the "good shepherd,"
the divine I AM.

7 Jesus therefore said unto them again, Verily, verily, I say unto you, I am the door of the sheep. 8 All that came before me are thieves and robbers: but the sheep did not hear them. 9 I am the door; by me if any man enter in, he shall be saved, and shall go in and go out, and shall find pasture. 10 The thief cometh not, but that he may steal, and kill, and destroy: I came that they may have life, and may have *it* abundantly. 11 I am the good shepherd: the good shepherd layeth down his life for the sheep. 12 He that is a hireling, and not a shepherd, whose own the sheep are not, beholdeth the wolf coming, and leaveth the sheep, and fleeth, and the wolf snatcheth them, and scattereth *them:* 13 *he fleeth because* he is a hireling; and careth not for the sheep. 14 I am the good shepherd; and I know mine own, and mine own know me, 15 even as the Father knoweth me, and I know the Father; and I lay down my life for the sheep. 16 And other sheep I have, which are not of this fold: them also I must bring, and they shall hear my voice; and they shall become one flock, one shepherd. 17 Therefore doth the Father love me, because I lay down my life, that I may take it again. 18 No one taketh *it* away from me, but I lay it down of myself. I have power to lay it down, and I have power to take it again. This commandment received I from my Father.

"The good shepherd layeth down his life for the sheep." This means that the high spiritual I AM lets itself become identified with the limitations of self-consciousness that it may lift all up to the spiritual plane. "I lay down my life, that I may take it again."

When we open the door of the mind by consciously affirming the presence and power of the divine I AM in our midst, there is a marriage or union of the higher forces in being with the lower, and we find that we are quickened in every part; the life of the I AM has been poured out for us. Thus Christ becomes the Saviour of the whole world, by pouring this higher spiritual energy (His blood) into human consciousness, which each must take for himself and identify himself with. The individual I AM is the only door through which it can get into our thoughts in a legitimate way. If it comes through mediumship or hypnotism or mental suggestion, without our willing co-operation, it is "a thief and a robber."

There is but one life-giver, one Saviour, the Christ; and the only door through which the divine essence can come to us is through our own I AM. Jesus of Nazareth points the way, but everyone must take up his cross and follow Him, must "overcome" as He overcame.

19 There arose a division again among the Jews because of these words. 20 And many of them said, He hath a demon, and is mad; why hear ye him? 21 Others said, These are not the sayings of one possessed with a demon. Can a demon open the eyes of the blind?

The word *Jews* in this instance refers to the Pharisaical Jews who are following the letter of the law. There is always a division among the intellectually wise and an arguing back and forth. It is the Christ consciousness alone that seeks the unity of all things.

22 And it was the feast of the dedication at Jeru-

salem: 23 it was winter; and Jesus was walking in
the temple in Solomon's porch.

Partaking of a feast in Solomon's Porch in the
Temple symbolizes our peaceful thought people ap-
propriating spiritual substance in an outer state of
consciousness (porch).

24 The Jews therefore came round about him,
and said unto him, How long dost thou hold us in
suspense? If thou art the Christ, tell us plainly. 25
Jesus answered them, I told you, and ye believe not:
the works that I do in my Father's name, these bear
witness of me. 26 But ye believe not, because ye are
not of my sheep.

In this Scripture Jesus symbolizes the I AM or
Christ, and the Jews symbolize our high-brow intellectual thoughts, which hold to the letter of the
law to such an extent that they cannot let the spiritual word expand in and through the consciousness.

27 My sheep hear my voice, and I know them,
and they follow me: 28 and I give unto them eternal
life; and they shall never perish, and no one shall
snatch them out of my hand. 29 My Father, who
hath given *them* unto me, is greater than all; and
no one is able to snatch *them* out of the Father's
hand. 30 I and the Father are one.

"My sheep hear my voice." The sheep are our
gentle, obedient thoughts that are always open to
the inspiration of the Christ. Man's soul is encased
in the body, with its great organ or instrument from
which issues forth the human voice. When man is

established in his I AM power and dominion, His voice is strong and vibrant and commanding. God revealed Himself to the prophets of old through the "still small voice." While it is not audible it is distinct and clear. Many ask how to distinguish the real voice. They hear voices and voices but do not understand how to distinguish the real one. If man follows the Holy Spirit, the one teacher, if he concentrates on the power of the word and holds continuously for the leading of the Spirit of truth, he will enter into a state of spiritual discernment in which he can readily distinguish the still small voice.

31 The Jews took up stones again to stone him. 32 Jesus answered them, Many good works have I showed you from the Father; for which of those works do ye stone me? 33 The Jews answered him, For a good work we stone thee not, but for blasphemy; and because that thou, being a man, makest thyself God. 34 Jesus answered them, Is it not written in your law, I said, Ye are gods? 35 If he called them gods, unto whom the word of God came (and the scripture cannot be broken), 36 say ye of him, whom the Father sanctified and sent into the world, Thou blasphemest; because I said, I am *the* Son of God? If I do not the works of my Father, believe me not. 38 But if I do them, though ye believe not me, believe the works: that ye may know and understand that the Father is in me, and I in the Father. 39 They sought again to take him: and he went forth out of their hand.

40 And he went away again beyond the Jordan into the place where John was at the first baptizing; and there he abode. 41 And many came unto him; and they said, John indeed did no sign: but all things whatsoever John spake of this man were

true. 42 And many believed on him there.

After the Christ has done a positive work it always withdraws to an inner state of consciousness in order to replenish its power before it goes forth to achieve again. Into this state of consciousness opposing intellect cannot find entrance. But after a season the Christ again penetrates into the Jordan or subconsciousness made up of thoughts good, bad, and indifferent. Here man is in an ignorant and unredeemed state. His concepts are turbulent with materiality. However here again the light of the Christ penetrates, and many believe and receive the Truth. Jesus has made conscious unity with His supermind or I AM mind and through it with the Father. This is the only way in which any man can attain perfection.

Here again Jesus emphasizes the importance of works to prove one's claims of spiritual authority and power. "If I do not the works of my Father, believe me not." The world is full of religious leaders who cannot do the works promised by Jesus, and yet they are accepted as His representative. He said, "These signs shall accompany them that believe."

# John: Chapter 11

Now a certain man was sick, Lazarus of Bethany, of the village of Mary and her sister Martha. 2 And it was that Mary who anointed the Lord with ointment, and wiped his feet with her hair, whose brother Lazarus was sick. 3 The sisters therefore sent unto him, saying, Lord, behold, he whom thou lovest is sick. 4 But when Jesus heard it, he said, This sickness is not unto death, but for the glory of God, that the Son of God may be glorified thereby. 5 Now Jesus loved Martha, and her sister, and Lazarus. 6 When therefore he heard that he was sick, he abode at that time two days in the place where he was. 7 Then after this he saith to the disciples, Let us go into Judæa again. 8 The disciples say unto him, Rabbi, the Jews were but now seeking to stone thee; and goest thou thither again? 9 Jesus answered, Are there not twelve hours in the day? If a man walk in the day, he stumbleth not, because he seeth the light of this world. 10 But if a man walk in the night, he stumbleth, because the light is not in him. 11 These things spake he: and after this he saith unto them, Our friend Lazarus is fallen asleep; but I go, that I may awake him out of sleep. 12 The disciples therefore said unto him, Lord, if he is fallen asleep, he will recover. 13 Now Jesus had spoken of his death: but they thought that he spake of taking rest in sleep. 14 Then Jesus therefore said unto them plainly, Lazarus is dead. 15 And I am glad for your sakes that I was not there, to the intent ye may believe; nevertheless let us go unto him. 16 Thomas therefore, who is called Didymus, said unto his fellow-disciples, Let us also go, that we may die with him.

THE NAME *Lazarus* means "whom God helps." Metaphysically interpreted, Lazarus represents the spiritual strength that comes to man through his recognition of God as his supporting, sustaining power. When man fails to recognize God as the origin and support of his life, spiritual understanding becomes weak in him and he sinks into materiality. To all intents he is dead to the Truth of his own being. The devotional soul, Mary, and the practical soul, Martha, are sisters in this intellect, and although like all women they have faith in the Spirit, they allow themselves to fall under the thought of mortal law and believe in the reality of death. The whole world is under the hypnotism of this material belief, and it is making tombs for thousands every day.

Out of a torpid condition of soul like that of Lazarus the I AM (Jesus) calls forth the living Spirit of the Christ, and reawakens by one word the consciousness of true understanding in man and the quickened perception of his faculties.

The name *Thomas* means "twin." Spiritually considered, Thomas is understanding, whose twin is Matthew, the will. Matthew, metaphysical twin of Thomas, is not so described in the Scriptures; spiritually he is identified as the co-ordinating faculty. In a well-balanced mind understanding is followed by action.

Intellectual understanding assures us of the truth of our sense impressions. It says, "Seeing is believing." According to this dictum, if we should see written on a blackboard, "Two plus two equals six," we should be called on to accept as true a contradiction of the principles of mathematics.

17 So when Jesus came, he found that he [Lazarus] had been in the tomb four days already. 18 Now Bethany was nigh unto Jerusalem, about fifteen furlongs off; 19 and many of the Jews had come to Martha and Mary, to console them concerning their brother. 20 Martha therefore, when she heard that Jesus was coming, went and met him: but Mary still sat in the house. 21 Martha therefore said unto Jesus, Lord, if thou hadst been here, my brother had not died. 22 And even now I know that, whatsoever thou shalt ask of God, God will give thee. 23 Jesus saith unto her, Thy brother shall rise again. 24 Martha saith unto him, I know that he shall rise again in the resurrection at the last day. 25 Jesus said unto her, I am the resurrection, and the life: he that believeth on me, though he die, yet shall he live; 26 and whosoever liveth and believeth on me shall never die. Believest thou this? 27 She saith unto him, Yea, Lord; I have believed that thou art the Christ, the Son of God, *even* he that cometh into the world. 28 And when she had said this, she went away, and called Mary her sister secretly, saying, The Teacher is here, and calleth thee. 29 And she, when she heard it, arose quickly, and went unto him. 30 (Now Jesus was not yet come into the village, but was still in the place where Martha met him.) 31 The Jews then who were with her in the house, and were consoling her, when they saw Mary, that she rose up quickly and went out, followed her, supposing that she was going unto the tomb to weep there. 32 Mary therefore, when she came where Jesus was, and saw him, fell down at his feet, saying unto him, Lord, if thou hadst been here, my brother had not died. 33 When Jesus therefore saw her weeping, and the Jews *also* weeping who came with her, he groaned in the spirit, and was troubled, 34 and said, Where have ye laid him? They say unto him, Lord,

come and see. 35 Jesus wept. 36 The Jews therefore said, Behold how he loved him! 37 But some of them said, Could not this man, who opened the eyes of him that was blind, have caused that this man also should not die? 38 Jesus therefore again groaning in himself cometh to the tomb. Now it was a cave, and a stone lay against it. 39 Jesus saith, Take ye away the stone. Martha, the sister of him that was dead, saith unto him, Lord, by this time the body decayeth; for he hath been *dead* four days. 40 Jesus saith unto her, Said I not unto thee, that, if thou believedst, thou shouldest see the glory of God? 41 So they took away the stone. And Jesus lifted up his eyes, and said, Father, I thank thee that thou heardest me. 42 And I knew that thou hearest me always: but because of the multitude that standeth around I said it, that they may believe that thou didst send me. 43 And when he had thus spoken, he cried with a loud voice, Lazarus, come forth. 44 He that was dead came forth, bound hand and foot with grave-clothes; and his face was bound about with a napkin. Jesus saith unto them, Loose him, and let him go.

Jesus represents man in the regeneration; that is, man in the process of restoring his body to its natural condition, where it will live right on perpetually without old age, disease, or death. A necessary step in this process of body restoration is the quickening of the sleeping Lazarus, who represents the vitalizing energies in the subconsciousness that feed the body and give it the life force that renews its youth.

Jesus was at Bethany near Jerusalem. Metaphysically Jerusalem represents a point in consciousness where the spiritual energy of life is strong enough to vitalize adjacent body substance (Bethany, "house

of figs"). Jesus vitalized and baptized His soul
and body with spirit life when He denied the power
of death over Lazarus and affirmed the resurrecting
life. We can do the same thing when we do it in His
name. Jesus' groaning and weeping represent the
seemingly insurmountable conditions that are just
before us.

We should ever remember that the youth we love
so well never dies; it is merely asleep in the subconscious—Jesus said that Lazarus was not dead.
People grow old because they let the youth idea fall
asleep. This idea is not dead but is sleeping, and the
understanding I AM (Jesus) goes to awaken it. This
awakening of youthful energies is necessary to one in
the regeneration. The body cannot be refined and
made, like its Creator, eternal before all the thoughts
necessary to its perpetuation are revived in it. Eternal
youth is one of these God-given ideas that man loves.
Jesus loved Lazarus.

The outer senses say that this vitalizing force
of youth is dead in man, that it has been dead for so
long that it has gone into dissolution, decay; but
the keener knowledge of the spiritual man proclaims, "Our friend Lazarus is fallen asleep; but I . . .
awake him out of sleep."

Bringing this sleeping life to outer consciousness
is no easy task. Jesus groaned in spirit and was
troubled at the prospect. The higher must enter into
sympathy and love with the lower to bring about the
awakening—"Jesus wept." But there must be more
than sympathy and love—"Take ye away the stone."
The "stone" that holds the sleeping life in the

tomb of matter in subconsciousness is the belief in the permanency of present material laws. This "stone" must be rolled away through faith. The man who wants the inner life to spring forth must believe in the reality of omnipresent spiritual life and must exercise his faith by invoking in prayer the presence of the invisible but omnipresent God. This reveals to consciousness the glory of Spirit, and the soul has witness in itself of a power that it knew not.

In Spirit all things are fulfilled now. The moment a concept enters the mind, the thing conceived is consummated through the law that governs the action of ideas. The inventor mentally sees his machine doing the work designed, though he may be years short of making it do that work. The spiritual-minded take advantage of this law and affirm the completeness of this ideal, regardless of outer appearances. This stimulates the energy in the thought process and gives it power beyond estimate. This is the step that Jesus took when He lifted up His eyes and said: "Father, I thank thee that thou heardest me. And I knew that thou hearest me always." The sleeping youth (Lazarus) does not at once respond, but the prayer of thanksgiving that is now in action gives the assurance that calls it at the next step to the surface—"Lazarus, come forth."

Jesus "cried with a loud voice." This emphasizes the necessity of working strenuously to project the inner life to the surface. Beginners find it easy, under proper instruction, to quicken the various life centers in the body and co-ordinate them as a body

battery that, under the direction of the will, throws
a current of energy to any desired place. A time comes
when the outer flesh must be vitalized with this inner life; then arises the necessity of using the "loud
voice" as the propelling force. This is removing
from the face the "napkin," which represents conscious intelligence made manifest.

Freedom from all trammels is necessary before
the imprisoned life can find its natural channel in
the constitution. "Loose him, and let him go" means
unfettered life expressing itself in joyous freedom
of Spirit. The flesh would take this vital flood and
use it in the old way, put new wine into old bottles,
but Spirit guides those who trust it, and leads them
in righteous ways when they listen patiently to the
inner guide.

This raising of Lazarus is performed every day by
those who are putting on the new Christ body
through the resurrected Christ life.

45 Many therefore of the Jews, who came to
Mary and beheld that which he did, believed on him.
46 But some of them went away to the Pharisees,
and told them the things which Jesus had done.

Interpreted within ourselves, there are always
the thought forces that believe the Truth and accept
the so-called miracles of the Christ, but there are
also those that question and resort to the Pharisees
(the strict intellectual phase of mind) for their
stamp of approval.

47 The chief priests therefore and the Pharisees

gathered a council, and said, What do we? for this man doeth many signs. 48 If we let him thus alone, all men will believe on him: and the Romans will come and take away both our place and our nation. 49 But a certain one of them, Caiaphas, being high priest that year, said unto them, Ye know nothing at all, 50 nor do ye take account that it is expedient for you that one man should die for the people, and that the whole nation perish not. 51 Now this he said not of himself: but being high priest that year, he prophesied that Jesus should die for the nation; 52 and not for the nation only, but that he might also gather together into one the children of God that are scattered abroad. 53 So from that day forth they took counsel that they might put him to death.

In this instance the Pharisees represent a congregation of intellectual thought people called together to counsel with one another. The Romans symbolize the rule of the natural man. The intellectual Pharisee is always jealous of his religious rights and fearful of being robbed of his own. He observes the forms of religion but neglects the spirit. He does not understand the activities of the Christ Mind and therefore fears it.

Another tendency of the intellect is to question and argue back and forth. The high priest symbolizes the highest spiritual thought force in authority that has an inkling of Truth, and he perceives that the Christ will eventually give His life for the redemption of all. The narrow intellect, however, does not have the spiritual viewpoint and seeks to destroy the saving spiritual power.

54 Jesus therefore walked no more openly among
the Jews, but departed thence into the country near
to the wilderness, into a city called Ephraim; and
there he tarried with the disciples. 55 Now the passover of the Jews was at hand: and many went up to
Jerusalem out of the country before the passover,
to purify themselves. 56 They sought therefore for
Jesus, and spake one with another, as they stood in
the temple, What think ye? That he will not come
to the feast? 57 Now the chief priests and the Pharisees had given commandment, that, if any man knew
where he was, he should show it, that they might
take him.

When a state of consciousness is not open to
Truth, the Christ (in this Scripture symbolized by
Jesus) withdraws to an inner sanctum (here symbolized by Ephraim, a name that means "doubly
fruitful"), where closer union with the great divine
source is found. Jesus therefore walked no more
openly among the Jews.

The Feast of the Passover represents a passing
from a lower state of consciousness to a higher. For
the spiritual passover the devout always seek the city
of peace (Jerusalem). No matter in what state of
consciousness one may be functioning there is always that within which craves something better. The
intellect, continuing to believe it is to be the highest
authority, would kill out the Christ.

# *John: Chapter 12*

Jesus therefore six days before the passover came
to Bethany, where Lazarus was, whom Jesus raised
from the dead. 2 So they made him a supper there:
and Martha served; but Lazarus was one of them
that sat at meat with him. 3 Mary therefore took a
pound of ointment of pure nard, very precious, and
anointed the feet of Jesus, and wiped his feet with
her hair: and the house was filled with the odor of
the ointment.

BETHANY MEANS "a place of fruits," dates,
bread, that is, substance. Whenever we make
a mental demonstration we get a certain
result in our body. This is called the "fruit" of our
thought.

When Jesus went to Bethany He realized the fruit
or effect of raising Lazarus; that is, the quickening
of certain sleeping energies in His body consciousness.

This realization is a feast to the soul and body, a
filling of the whole man with a sense of satisfaction.
Martha, the practical soul, and Mary, the devotional,
serve the Master. Martha provides the material ne-
cessities and Mary the spiritual, while Lazarus sits
at meat (abides as the living substance of the subconsciousness).

Mary, the devotional side of the soul, is grateful
for the awakening of her brother Lazarus, because
she depends for her manifestation on the subconscious life that he represents. When the soul is
lifted up in prayer and thanksgiving, there follows
an outflow of love that fills the whole "house" or
body with its odor. The anointing of Jesus' feet represents the willingness of love to serve. When Jesus

washed the feet of His apostles He said, "He that
is . . . greater among you, let him become as the
younger; and he that is chief, as he that doth serve."

4 But Judas Iscariot, one of his disciples, that
should betray him, saith, 5 Why was not this ointment sold for three hundred shillings, and given
to the poor? 6 Now this he said, not because he cared
for the poor; but because he was a thief, and having
the bag took away what was put therein. 7 Jesus
therefore said, suffer her to keep it against the day
of my burying. 8 For the poor ye have always with
you; but me ye have not always.

9 The common people therefore of the Jews
learned that he was there: and they came, not for
Jesus' sake only, but that they might see Lazarus also,
whom he had raised from the dead. 10 But the
chief priests took counsel that they might put Lazarus also to death; 11 because that by reason of him
many of the Jews went away, and believed on Jesus.

Judas Iscariot (sense consciousness) is incarnated
selfishness, and his every thought is to build up personality. When Mary anoints the feet of Jesus (when
love pours out her precious substance, diffusing its
essence throughout the whole man), Judas inquires
why the ointment was not sold and the proceeds
given to the poor. The Judas consciousness believes
in poverty and has no understanding of the true law
of supply. All that comes into consciousness is selfish-
ly appropriated and dissipated by this thief, yet he
produces nothing. Sense consciousness is the enig-
ma of existence, and in it is wrapped up the mystery
of individuality. Jesus knew that through this department of His being He would be betrayed, but

He made no effort to defeat the act of Judas. Sense consciousness betrays man every day, yet it would be unwise wholly to destroy it before its time, because at its foundation it is good; it has simply gone wrong; it "hath a devil."

Love is the "greatest thing in the world," according to Henry Drummond, who analyzed it in a masterly manner. Jesus acknowledged the power of love when He said, "Suffer her to keep it against the day of my burying." When personality is hurt to the death and surrenders all, love pours her balm over every wound and the substance of her sympathy infuses hope and faith into the discouraged soul. A noted mental healer relates that her husband was dying of consumption. She had treated him in every way known to her science without results, when one day in her agony she exclaimed, "I will give my whole life to save you." Immediately, she says, a great flood of substance seemed to roll forth from her heart toward her husband, and from that day he began to improve, and he finally got well. This was the precious ointment of love, poured out for him when he was buried in the consciousness of death, and it resurrected him. Divine Love hath a balm for every ill.

12 On the morrow a great multitude that had come to the feast, when they heard that Jesus was coming to Jerusalem, 13 took the branches of the palm trees, and went forth to meet him, and cried out, Hosanna: Blessed *is* he that cometh in the name of the Lord, even the King of Israel. 14 And Jesus, having found a young ass, sat thereon; as it is written,

15 Fear not, daughter of Zion: behold, thy King cometh, sitting on an ass's colt. 16 These things understood not his disciples at the first: but when Jesus was glorified, then remembered they that these things were written of him, and that they had done these things unto him. 17 The multitude therefore that was with him when he called Lazarus out of the tomb, and raised him from the dead, bare witness. 18 For this cause also the multitude went and met him, for that they heard that he had done this sign. 19 The Pharisees therefore said among themselves, Behold how ye prevail nothing; lo, the world is gone after him.

The triumphal entry of Jesus into Jerusalem and His reception by the multitude represents a transient and external enthusiasm, the result of demonstrations in the outer. This multitude that went forth to meet Him, crying, "Hosanna: Blessed *is* he that cometh in the name of the Lord," did so because they had witnessed the raising of Lazarus. Their homage to Jesus was based on the "signs" that they had witnessed, and not on that deep inner conviction of Truth that attests the sincere followers.

A large proportion of those who espouse the cause in this day do so from the "signs" standpoint. They have observed some demonstration, and accept the philosophy as they would a new patent medicine, and they change their doctrine as readily as the doser does his drug.

20 Now there were certain Greeks among those that went up to worship at the feast: 21 these therefore came to Philip, who was of Bethsaida of Galilee, and asked him, saying, Sir, we would see Jesus.

22 Philip cometh and telleth Andrew: Andrew cometh, and Philip, and they tell Jesus. 23 And Jesus answereth them, saying, The hour is come, that the Son of man should be glorified. 24 Verily, verily, I say unto you, Except a grain of wheat fall into the earth and die, it abideth by itself alone; but if it die, it beareth much fruit. 25 He that loveth his life loseth it; and he that hateth his life in this world shall keep it unto life eternal. 26 If any man serve me, let him follow me; and where I am, there shall also my servant be: if any man serve me, him will the Father honor.

Common sense often saves a man from the fanaticism of religious enthusiasm. The Greeks represent the practical side of man's nature. They ask Philip for an interview with Jesus, and Philip tells Andrew. All this means that it is through the power (Philip) and strength (Andrew) in man that the sense reason acts, and when the I AM is called down from its lofty spiritual enthronement to the contemplation of practical life, there is a restoration of equilibrium. Then it recognizes the law of giving its exalted ideality to the earthly consciousness, that it may also be lifted up. To the higher consciousness this seems like the death of an ideal, but it is only a temporary submergence, which has its resurrection in a great increase of life and power. Thus we lose our life in the service of the good, and count it of no value in order to find it again in Spirit.

27 Now is my soul troubled; and what shall I say? Father, save me from this hour. But for this cause came I unto this hour. 28 Father, glorify thy

name. There came therefore a voice out of heaven, *saying,* I have both glorified it, and will glorify it again. 29 The multitude therefore, that stood by, and heard it, said that it had thundered: others said, An angel hath spoken to him. 30 Jesus answered and said, This voice hath not come for my sake, but for your sakes.

Jesus' mission on earth was to save the race from bondage, from sin, sickness, and death. This Scripture reveals that Jesus had been able to realize the Truth in this regard and that the time was now approaching for the demonstration. In the face of it all, He realized He was on new ground and there was that within Him which was troubled. "Father, save me from this hour. But for this cause came I unto this hour. Father, glorify thy name." From within Him came the reassuring voice of God: "I have both glorified it [the name] and will glorify it again." This means that Jesus' heavenly credentials were sufficient and that there was nothing to fear. The demonstration must eventually be forthcoming.

31 Now is the judgment of this world: now shall the prince of this world be cast out. 32 And I, if I be lifted up from the earth, will draw all men unto myself. 33 But this he said, signifying by what manner of death he should die. 34 The multitude therefore answered him, We have heard out of the law that the Christ abideth for ever: and how sayest thou, The Son of man must be lifted up? who is this Son of man? 35 Jesus therefore said unto them, Yet a little while is the light among you. Walk while ye have the light, that darkness overtake you not: and he that walketh in the darkness knoweth not whither he goes. 36 While ye have the light,

believe on the light, that ye may become sons of
light.

The multitude here referred to is the multitude
of thoughts within the soul that is endeavoring to
lay hold of the laws of spirituality. Jesus' admonition was "Yet a little while is the light among you.
Walk while ye have the light, that darkness overtake
you not."

36 These things spake Jesus, and he departed and
hid himself from them. 37 But though he had done
so many signs before them, yet they believed not
on him: 38 that the word of Isaiah the prophet
might be fulfilled, which he spake,
Lord, who hath believed our report?
And to whom hath the arm of the Lord been revealed?
39 For this cause they could not believe, for that
Isaiah said again,
40 He hath blinded their eyes, and he hardened
their heart;
Lest they should see with their eyes, and perceive
with their heart,
And should turn,
And I should heal them.
41 These things said Isaiah, because he saw his
glory; and he spake of him. 42 Nevertheless even of
the rulers many believed on him; but because of the
Pharisees they did not confess *it,* lest they should be
put out of the synagogue: 43 for they loved the glory
*that is* of men more than the glory *that is* of God.

By a "prophet" within the soul is understood the
capacity to read out of the law and to perceive to
what degree the soul can really demonstrate spirituality. It is revealed that in this Scripture the Phari-

saical intellect was in authority, compelling the soul
forces that were beginning to understand Truth
but that still loved the glory that is of men more
than the glory that is of God to do obeisance to it.

44 And Jesus cried and said, He that believeth
on me, believeth not on me, but on him that sent me.
45 And he that beholdeth me beholdeth him that
sent me. 46 I am come a light into the world, that
whosoever believeth on me may not abide in the darkness. 47 And if any man hear my sayings, and keep
them not, I judge him not: for I came not to judge
the world, but to save the world. 48 He that rejecteth
me, and receiveth not my sayings, hath one that judgeth him: the word that I spake, the same shall judge
him in the last day. 49 For I spake not from myself; but the Father that sent me, he hath given me
a commandment, what I should say, and what I
should speak. 50 And I know that his commandment
is life eternal; the things therefore which I speak,
even as the Father hath said unto me, so I speak.

In this Scripture Jesus (symbolizing the indwelling Christ) is declaring to the whole soul consciousness that the preponderance of power is spiritual.
Spiritual character is the rock foundation of Being;
therefore He is urging the multitude of thoughts to
realize that their redemption comes through de-
creeing their oneness with Spirit and that the will
of God is active in consciousness.

The realization of divine unity is the highest
that we may attain. This is true glory, the blending
and merging of the whole being in Divine Mind.
"Build yourself into God and you will find yourself
in heaven right here and now."

# John: Chapter 13

Now before the feast of the passover, Jesus
knowing that his hour was come that he should depart out of this world unto the Father, having loved
his own that were in the world, he loved them unto
the end. 2 And during supper, the devil having already put into the heart of Judas Iscariot, Simon's
*son,* to betray him, 3 *Jesus,* knowing that the Father
had given all things into his hands, and that he came
forth from God, and goeth unto God, 4 riseth from
supper, and layeth aside his garments; and he took
a towel, and girded himself. 5 Then he poureth water
into the basin, and began to wash the disciples' feet,
and to wipe them with the towel wherewith he was
girded.

WE HAVE PROOF on every side that through
our mind we are unified into the one
Mind. Through the interflowing of mind
and Mind we act and react on each other, and
"no man liveth unto himself alone." By this mind
contact we all become responsible for the good or
bad conditions in our neighbors and remotely for
that of the whole race. Christianity teaches that sin
came into the world through the sin of one man,
Adam, and that it is cast out by the righteousness
of one man, Jesus. This was demonstrated by the
projection into the race consciousness of the blood
or spiritually quickened life energy of Jesus as a
solvent for sin.

Satan represents the adverse ego in the race
that opposes and resists the divine law, and Judas
is its personal representative. Jesus purified all
the elements composing His blood, smashed the
atoms and released the electrons into the race con-

sciousness, subjecting them to the will and appropriation of anyone who exercises sufficient faith and the desire to attain that end. Giving up this life essence was a great sacrifice on the part of Jesus; it was trusting to others His very life essence to be appropriated by them and restored to Him when all have attained the purity of the principles that it represents.

In this episode Jesus is about to make the great sacrifice; the passing over from one state of consciousness to another is about to take place. Then He ceases to be the great leader of men and through surrender of the most precious possession of man, his life, Jesus becomes the lowly servant of us all.

By His acts Jesus taught as many lessons in soul unfoldment as by His words. Soul unfoldment means the bringing forth of divine ideas in the soul or consciousness of man and the bringing of these ideas into expression in the body. Jesus told His disciples that those who would become truly great must serve. Those who have become great have first learned, as a matter of course, to serve and in so doing have found their own good.

The undisciplined disciples had disputed about who should have the higher places in the kingdom, who should be the greatest, who should sit at the right hand of the Master and who at the left. Jesus cited to them the little child's guilelessness and trustfulness and willingness to learn. He also showed them the difference between divine greatness and the human idea of greatness. Finally He told them that whoever would be great among them should be their minister or servant, even as the Son of man came to minister and to "give his life a ransom for many." To have everything done for one is to remain a child, but to do for others is to reach man's estate. Jesus gave His very life in service to the world, and He left us an example that we should follow. We should be eager to become as unselfishly humble and willing to minister to others for their eternal good as He was.

6 So he cometh to Simon Peter. He saith unto him, Lord, dost thou wash my feet? 7 Jesus answered and said unto him, What I do thou knowest not now; but thou shalt understand hereafter. 8 Peter saith unto him, Thou shalt never wash my feet. Jesus answered him, If I wash thee not, thou hast no part with me. 9 Simon Peter saith unto him, Lord, not my feet only, but also my hands and my head. 10 Jesus saith to him, He that is bathed needeth not save to wash his feet, but is clean every whit: and ye are clean, but not all. 11 For he knew him that should betray him; therefore said he, Ye are not all clean.

12 So when he had washed their feet, and taken his garments, and sat down again, he said unto them, Know ye what I have done to you? 13 Ye call me, Teacher, and, Lord: and ye say well; for so I am. 14 If I then, the Lord and the Teacher, have washed your feet, ye also ought to wash one another's feet. 15 For I have given you an example, that ye also should do as I have done to you. 16 Verily, verily, I say unto you, A servant is not greater than his lord; neither one that is sent greater than he that sent him. 17 If ye know these things, blessed are ye if ye do them.

Spiritual consciousness puts all men and all things

on a common level. In the sight of God there is
no great, no small. The principle of life (that is,
God immanent in the universe as the great under-
lying cause of all manifestation) supplies the humble, unlearned laborer as fully and as freely as it supplies the most cultured person. Those who "put . . .
on . . . Christ" (develop a consciousness according
to the Christ standard) disregard rank and title.

Some years ago two humble missionary workers
who had been in China were received into the home
of a wealthy woman in America who was interested
in foreign missions. When the hour of departure
came, they walked two blocks to the elevated train
to save taxi fare. Their hostess, who lived simply
and did not even keep an automobile, insisted on ac-
companying them to the station and helped them
carry their hand baggage. She had given millions to
the cause of health and education in India and China,
yet she was completely democratic and simple.

The feet are the willing and patient servants of
the body. They go all day at the bidding of the
mind, and upon them rest many of the burdens that
result from material thoughts. The more we believe
in the false importance of matter the greater is
the burden laid upon our feet and the more tired they
become.

By washing the feet of His apostles Jesus denied
the race idea of matter as all-important and taught
the value of service. Even Peter (spiritual faith) had
to be cleansed of his belief in the seeming reality
of material conditions. It seems a menial thing to
wash another's feet, but Jesus taught and exemplified

the willingness of divine love to serve in humble ways and thus redeem man from the pride of the flesh.

As through His great love Jesus cleansed our understanding, so should we cleanse the understanding of our fellows. He delegates to His disciples and students of every age and land the power to cleanse man's mind of false standards of life. This Christ cleansing through love is not only a teaching; it is also a life to be lived. The true teacher of practical Christianity must be a Christian, a follower of Jesus in all His ways. Those who, like Judas, are possessed of the adverse mind should receive the same humble service, the same lesson that is given to persons who are true and faithful.

18 I speak not of you all: I know whom I have chosen: but that the scripture may be fulfilled, He that eateth my bread lifted up his heel against me. 19 From henceforth I tell you before it come to pass, that, when it is come to pass, ye may believe that I am *he*. 20 Verily, verily, I say unto you, He that receiveth whomsoever I send receiveth me; and he that receiveth me receiveth him that sent me.

21 When Jesus had thus said, he was troubled in the spirit, and testified, and said, Verily, verily, I say unto you, that one of you shall betray me. 22 The disciples looked one on another, doubting of whom he spake. 23 There was at the table reclining in Jesus' bosom one of his disciples, whom Jesus loved. 24 Simon Peter therefore beckoneth to him, and saith unto him, Tell *us* who it is of whom he speaketh. 25 He leaning back, as he was, on Jesus' breast saith unto him, Lord, who is it? 26 Jesus therefore answereth, He it is, for whom I shall dip the sop, and give it him. So when he had dipped the sop, he

taketh and giveth it to Judas, *the son* of Simon
Iscariot. 27 And after the sop, then entered Satan into
him. Jesus therefore saith unto him, What thou
doest, do quickly. 28 Now no man at the table
knew for what intent he spake this unto him. 29 For
some thought, because Judas had the bag, that Jesus
said unto him, Buy what things we have need of for
the feast; or, that he should give something to the
poor. 30 He then having received the sop went out
straightway: and it was night.

The Christ symbolized by Jesus is eternally the
I AM, though the disciples may not fully understand.
The Judas faculty, the sum of the unredeemed life
forces, is bound to betray until it is spiritualized.
Jesus (the Christ) knew that this unredeemed condition was bound to bring about tragedy. The physical
life represented by Judas may be ambitious, selfish,
proud, tyrannical, but we cannot do without it. The
false must be overcome. When faith and love ask
questions the way for illumination and revelation is
opened.

31 When therefore he was gone out, Jesus saith,
Now is the Son of man glorified, and God is glorified in him, 32 and God shall glorify him in himself,
and straightway shall he glorify him. 33 Little children, yet a little while I am with you. Ye shall seek
me: and as I said unto the Jews, Whither I go, ye
cannot come; so now I say unto you. 34 A new commandment I give unto you, that ye love one another; even as I have loved you, that ye also love one
another. 35 By this shall all men know that ye are
my disciples, if ye have love one to another.

When a soul makes complete union with God-

Mind there is always an outpouring of the Holy
Spirit upon it. This is true glorification, the acknowledgment by the Father that the Son is indeed lifted
up (glorified).

Jesus at this point was in a high spiritual state
of consciousness; in fact, He had made a perfect at-
one-ment with the Father. He was aware that even
His apostles had not attained His glory. In the
meantime love is the great harmonizer, and finally
love is the fulfillment of the law.

> 36 Simon Peter saith unto him, Lord, whither
> goest thou? Jesus answered, Whither I go, thou canst
> not follow me now; but thou shalt follow afterwards.
> 37 Peter saith unto him, Lord, why cannot I follow
> thee even now? I will lay down my life for thee.
> 38 Jesus answereth, Wilt thou lay down thy life for
> me? Verily, verily, I say unto thee, The cock shall
> not crow, till thou hast denied me thrice.

When Jesus said that He was going away, Peter
said he wanted to go with Him. He said he would
lay down his life for Jesus. But the Master's insight
into the state of consciousness represented by Peter
gave Him foreknowledge of what would happen.
He warned Peter of his coming failure, and He
was prepared for the confusion and scattering of the
disciples. He knew that eventually Peter would
regain and express the Christ faith and that His
band of followers would preserve Christianity for
posterity but first they must be spiritually unfolded
as He was.

# John: Chapter 14

Let not your heart be troubled: believe in God, believe also in me. 2 In my Father's house are many mansions; if it were not so, I would have told you; for I go to prepare a place for you. 3 And if I go and prepare a place for you, I come again, and will receive you unto myself; that where I am, *there* ye may be also.

WE BELIEVE IN God. It follows logically that we believe also in the manifestation of God, the ideal man. This proposition once accepted, there dawns on the understanding the truth of an intimate relation existing between Father and Son. The Father, God, "Spirit," is within the Son as the animating principle. The full recognition by man of this indwelling Spirit, as it was in Jesus, makes man the central figure and ruling power in the manifest universe. "The kingdom of God is within you."

"Many mansions" means many abiding places. "Mansion" comes from the Latin *manere,* to remain. The meaning of Jesus was that He was making a permanent abiding place for those who believed in His teaching and accepted Him for what He really was—God manifest. The idea usually held out is that Jesus was preceding His disciples to heaven, where He would await and welcome them. But there is no such meaning in the text. The permanent abiding place to which Jesus invites His friends is "prepared" by Him: He makes the place Himself, in fact He is the place. "Where I am, *there* ye may be also:

4 And whither I go, ye know the way. 5 Thomas

saith unto him, Lord, we know not whither thou
goest; how know we the way? 6 Jesus saith unto him,
I am the way, and the truth, and the life: no one
cometh unto the Father, but by me. 7 If ye had
known me, ye would have known my Father also:
from henceforth ye know him, and have seen him. 8
Philip saith unto him, Lord, show us the Father,
and it sufficeth us. 9 Jesus saith unto him, Have I been
so long time with you, and dost thou not know me,
Philip? he that hath seen me hath seen the Father;
how sayest thou, Show us the Father? 10 Believest
thou not that I am in the Father, and the Father in
me? the words that I say unto you I speak not from
myself: but the Father abiding in me doeth his
works. 11 Believe me that I am in the Father, and
the Father in me: or else believe me for the very
works' sake.

"Whither I go, ye know the way." The intellectual man, Thomas, claims ignorance and says he
does not know the place or the way. Then Jesus
reveals the spiritual Truth to which He has gradually
been leading their minds, saying, "I am the way,
and the truth, and the life: no one cometh unto the
Father, but by me." An understanding of man's
spiritual nature reveals his unity with the omnipresent principle of life, the Father. Jesus the Christ
is in the Father, and the Father is in man. Whoever
sees the spirituality of man in himself or others sees
the Father. The Father principle may be so developed in man that it will move him unerringly in all
his ways, and the Father may even speak words
through his mouth. When this point is reached the
question of man's unity with the Father principle is
wholly removed, the manifestation of wisdom and

power in him proving that a higher principle is at work through him. "Believe me for the very works' sake."

But Philip (the power of the word) says, "Show us the Father." This faculty must be raised to the realization of the omnipresence of Spirit by an acknowledgment that the word of the I AM spoken through it is not of the mortal but of God. "The words that I say unto you I speak not of myself: but the Father abiding in me, doeth his works."

> 12 Verily, verily, I say unto you, He that believeth on me, the works that I do shall he do also; and greater *works* than these shall he do; because I go unto the Father. 13 And whatsoever ye shall ask in my name, that will I do, that the Father may be glorified in the Son. 14 If ye shall ask anything in my name, that will I do.

"Whatsoever ye shall ask in my name, that will I do." There is no limit here. "Whatsoever" covers everything. Then why do we not receive at all times when we ask in His name? Because we have not demonstrated the power of His name. The name stands for the spiritual man, and it is this name or sign of God with us that rewards our faith. Had we a check signed by a well-known financier we should not hesitate to present it at the bank and get the money. The same confidence in the life-giving and success-producing power of the risen Christ must be established in us. When we reach out into the great invisible spiritual substance all about us and think of ourselves as its expression, confidently expecting it to manifest itself through us, it will do so. If at the first trial we do not succeed, let us keep trying until we do succeed; for the promise can be proved true, "If ye shall ask anything in my name, that will I do."

15 If ye love me, ye will keep my commandments. 16 And I will pray the Father, and he shall give you another Comforter, that he may be with you for ever, 17 *even* the Spirit of truth: whom the world cannot receive; for it beholdeth him not, neither knoweth him: ye know him; for he abideth with you, and shall be in you. 18 I will not leave you desolate: I come unto you. 19 Yet a little while, and the world beholdeth me no more; but ye behold me: because I live, ye shall live also. 20 In that day ye shall know that I am in my Father, and ye in me, and I in you. 21 He that hath my commandments, and keepeth them, he it is that loveth me: and he that loveth me shall be loved of my Father, and I will love him, and will manifest myself unto him. 22 Judas (not Iscariot) saith unto him, Lord, what is come to pass that thou wilt manifest thyself unto us, and not unto the world? 23 Jesus answered and said unto him, If a man love me, he will keep my word: and my Father will love him, and we will come unto him, and make our abode with him. 24 He that loveth me not keepeth not my words: and the word which ye hear is not mine, but the Father's who sent me.

In this Scripture Jesus, representing the I AM, gives assurance of divine co-operation to those who are loyal in thought and word to the Truth. You now know the relation in which you stand to the Father. Spiritually you are one, but to sustain this spiritual relation until it is fully manifested in your body and environment requires attention. The concrete aspect of Truth, represented by the personality of Jesus, must be taken away before you can understand Truth in its abstract or universal sense. Then withdrawing your attention from the letter or personality and centering it on Truth in its spiritual essence, you find that there is an intelligible side to that which seems vague and indefinite. The Comforter, the Advocate, the Spirit of truth is omnipresent as divine wisdom and power, which are brought into active touch with our consciousness through our believing in Him. In "the world"—on the phenomenal side—we cannot know this guide and helper, but having learned the truth about the omnipresence of Spirit, with all the abundance of life, love, Truth, and intelligence through which it is made manifest, we at once begin to realize that the Mighty One dwells with us, and "shall be in you."

The going away of the I AM was apparent to sense consciousness only—the "world beholdeth me no more"—but the larger range of consciousness beholds an expansion of the sense of divine identity and life, "Ye behold me: because I live, ye shall live also." With this expansion of the sense of our divine identity comes a perception of our unity with the Father, and the absolute identity of our sense-limited I with the universal I AM, the Christ. "In that day ye shall know that I am in my Father, and ye in me, and I in you."

The question is frequently asked, Is it not presumptuous for us, who have at first no realization of their truth, to make the statements that Jesus made? No, it is not; because in Spirit we are all that He claimed for Himself, and in no other way except affirming this truth can we make it manifest. All who experiment with words find that they generate force in the mind and eventually affect the body. Jesus urged His disciples to believe on Him, to keep His commandments, His sayings, His words, and they went forth and did wonderful works in "the name of . . . Jesus Christ."

In this Scripture Jesus says that those who keep His commandments thus show their love for Him and that He will love them and manifest Himself to them. Understanding as we do the affinity that similar thoughts have for one another, we perceive why keeping "my word" and believing "in me" were so powerfully urged by Jesus. He transcended men in His high statements, and His work corresponded to them, and knowing this law that like thoughts and words swiftly seek unity, He took advantage of it to lift us all up to His high standard.

But we must get out of the "world" or letter before we can touch this spiritual potency. Judas asked why it was that Jesus would manifest Himself to them and not to the world. Jesus' answer is right in line with this mental law of words by which the speaker is put in contact with those who have uttered similar words: "If a man love me, he will keep my word: and my Father will love him, and we will come unto him, and make our abode with him. He that loveth me not keepeth not my words: and the word which ye hear is not mine, but the Father's who sent me."

25 These things have I spoken unto you, while *yet* abiding with you. 26 But the Comforter, *even* the Holy Spirit, whom the Father will send in my name, he shall teach you all things, and bring to your remembrance all that I said unto you. 27 Peace I leave with you; my peace I give unto you: not as the world giveth, give I unto you. Let not your heart be troubled, neither let it be fearful. 28 Ye heard how I said to you, I go away, and I come unto you. If ye loved me, ye would have rejoiced, because I go unto the Father: for the Father is greater than I. 29 And now I have told you before it come to pass, that, when it is come to pass, ye may believe. 30 I will no more speak much with you, for the prince of the world cometh: and he hath nothing in me; 31 but that the world may know that I love the Father, and as the Father gave me commandment, even so I do. Arise, let us go hence.

The Father is principle. The Son is this Father principle revealed in a creative plan. The Holy Spirit is the executive power of both Father and Son.

The Holy Spirit is not all of Being, nor the fullness of Christ, but an emanation or "breath" sent forth to do a divine work. Thus circumscribed, the Holy Spirit may in a sense be said to take on the characteristics of personality, but personality that for capacity transcends all man's conceptions.

The Holy Spirit was before the time of Jesus. However Jesus' life and demonstration gave a new impetus to it. The Holy Spirit or Spirit of truth is man's one sure guide in his spiritual ongoing. An outpouring of the Holy Spirit always brings peace and infinite faith in the Father through the Son.

(See John 15:17-27 for further interpretation.)

# John: Chapter 15

I am the true vine, and my Father is the husband-
man. 2 Every branch in me that beareth not fruit,
he taketh it away: and every *branch* that beareth
fruit, he cleanseth it, that it may bear more fruit.

METAPHYSICALLY stated, the Father is the
God-Mind; Jesus is the individual incarnation of that Mind, here called the true
vine. "Every branch in me" means the faculties of
mind, and the "fruit" is the thought.

The law is that an unused faculty atrophies
and withers away. This is true of everything in existence. Inertia and nonuse soon bring stagnation,
corruption, death, and disintegration. We have accepted this so universally as a fact of nature that
its original character as an intelligent force has
been overlooked. All the teaching of the Scriptures
is that a failure to use a talent or faculty meets
with a reprimand from the Father-Mind. The over-
careful servant who buried his talent had it taken
away from him and given to the one who had increased his the most. This also has been observed
in its negative aspect—a faculty overused draws its
vitality from the others and eventually depletes
them seriously, unless they are developed by bal-
anced exercise. This is a law of our being, and we
should regard it as an intelligent principle instead
of a blind force, as we usually do.

3 Already ye are clean because of the word
which I have spoken unto you. 4 Abide in me, and
I in you. As the branch cannot bear fruit of itself,

except it abide in the vine; so neither can ye, except
ye abide in me. 5 I am the vine, ye are the branches:
He that abideth in me, and I in him, the same beareth much fruit: for apart from me ye can do nothing.
6 If a man abide not in me, he is cast forth as a
branch, and it is withered; and they gather them, and
cast them into the fire, and they are burned. 7 If ye
abide in me, and my words abide in you, ask whatsoever ye will, and it shall be done unto you. 8
Herein is my Father glorified, that ye bear much
fruit; and *so* shall ye be my disciples. 9 Even as the
Father hath loved me, I also have loved you: abide
ye in my love. 10 If ye keep my commandments, ye
shall abide in my love; even as I have kept my
Father's commandments, and abide in his love. 11
These things have I spoken unto you, that my joy
may be in you, and *that* your joy may be made full.
12 This is my commandment, that ye love one another, even as I have loved you.

The soul in conscious touch with the Father-
Mind and striving to fulfill the divine law brings
the power of true words to bear in the purifying
and cleansing of its faculties. "Ye are clean because
of the word which I have spoken unto you." The
necessity of abiding in the I AM in order to bear
much fruit is affirmed. When our faith attaches itself to outer things, instead of the spiritual I AM,
it ceases to draw vitality from the one and only
source of all life, divine Principle. The only door
to this life is the I AM. This abiding is a conscious
centering of the mind in the depths within us by
means of repeated affirmations of our faith and
trust in it. This day-by-day repeating of affirmations finally opens a channel of intelligent communi-

cation with the silent forces at the depths of Being, thoughts and words flow forth from there, and an entirely new source of power is developed in the man.

When the thought or "word" of Truth from the supreme I AM of consciousness, becomes an abiding fact in our mind, we need no longer strive in external ways; we have but to express a deep desire in the soul and it is fulfilled. "Ask whatsoever ye will, and it shall be done unto you."

This constant affirming, with faith in the I AM within us, more and more establishes us in command of the real forces of Being. The abiding in the Spirit opens up the various spiritual powers one after the other. Love is a great force that dissolves all the opposers of true thought and thus smooths all the obstacles of life. This leads to joy, another positive force that has not been bearing fruit because of the obstructions heaped upon it by our failure to fulfill the law of All-Good. This wonderful kingdom within the soul is developed through the keeping of the "commandments"; that is, the commanding, controlling, and directing of every thought according to the harmonious law of love toward others. There is no occult mystery connected with this development of the soul forces; it is simply thinking and acting in terms of the law of love in our intercourse with our fellow men.

13 Greater love hath no man than this, that a man lay down his life for his friends. 14 Ye are my friends, if ye do the things which I command you. 15 No longer do I call you servants; for the servant

knoweth not what his lord doeth: but I have called you friends; for all things that I heard from my Father I have made known unto you. 16 Ye did not choose me, but I chose you, and appointed you, that ye should go and bear fruit, and *that* your fruit should abide: that whatsoever ye shall ask of the Father in my name, he may give it you.

In this Scripture we see Jesus realizing that His apostles had made wonderful progress and were functioning on the spiritual plane. Therefore, He no longer considered them of the world but knew definitely that henceforth they were to do the works of Him that sent them. As co-workers with Him, He called them "friends." In all His ministry Jesus taught freedom of the individual. We are not "servants" but agents free to do as we will.

17 These things I command you, that ye may love one another. 18 If the world hateth you, ye know that it hath hated me before *it hated* you. 19 If ye were of the world, the world would love its own: but because ye are not of the world, but I chose you out of the world, therefore the world hateth you. 20 Remember the word that I said unto you, A servant is not greater than his lord. If they persecuted me, they will also persecute you; if they kept my word, they will keep yours also. 21 But all these things will they do unto you for my name's sake, because they know not him that sent me. 22 If I had not come and spoken unto them, they had not had sin: but now they have no excuse for their sin. 23 He that hateth me hateth my Father also. 24 If I had not done among them the works which none other did, they had not had sin: but now have they both seen and hated both me and my Father. 25 But *this cometh to pass,* that the word may be fulfilled that

is written in their law, They hated me without a cause. 26 But when the Comforter is come, whom I will send unto you from the Father, *even* the Spirit of truth, which proceedeth from the Father, he shall bear witness of me: 27 and ye also bear witness, because ye have been with me from the beginning.

The Comforter or Holy Spirit is the law of God in action, and when thought of in this way it appears to have personality. From this truth the Hebrews got their conception of the personal, tribal God.

The functions ascribed to the Holy Comforter or Holy Spirit or Spirit of truth imply distinct personal subsistence: He is said to speak, search, select, reveal, reprove, testify, lead, comfort, distribute to every man, know the deep things of God, and He can be known by man only through his spiritual nature.

(See John 14:25-31 for further interpretation.)

# *John: Chapter 16*

These things have I spoken unto you, that ye should not be caused to stumble. 2 They shall put you out of the synagogues: yea, the hour cometh, that whosoever killeth you shall think that he offereth service unto God. 3 And these things will they do, because they have not known the Father, nor me. 4 But these things have I spoken unto you, that when their hour is come, ye may remember, how that I told you. And these things I said not unto you from the beginning, because I was with you. 5 But now I go unto him that sent me; and none of you asketh me, Whither goest thou? 6 But because I have spoken these things unto you, sorrow hath filled your heart.

JUST AS JESUS knew He was persecuted and would be persecuted so He knew that His followers would be persecuted. The ignorant persecute those whom they do not understand or revere.

The Pharisaical or worldly state of mind has no conception of the higher realm within but thinks it governs the whole man and is jealous of any attempt to usurp its power. Hence persecution follows.

While Jesus knew that His apostles did not fully comprehend all that He said, He was encouraging them to go forth in their spiritual strength and to travel the road that was ahead of them.

7 Nevertheless I tell you the truth: It is expedient for you that I go away; for if I go not away, the Comforter will not come unto you; but if I go, I will send him unto you. 8 And he, when he is come, will convict the world in respect of sin, and of right-

eousness, and of judgment: 9 of sin, because they
believe not on me; 10 of righteousness, because I
go to the Father, and ye behold me no more; 11 of
judgment, because the prince of this world hath been
judged. 12 I have yet many things to say unto you,
but ye cannot bear them now. 13 Howbeit when he,
the Spirit of truth, is come, he shall guide you into
all the truth: for he shall not speak from himself;
but what things soever he shall hear, these shall
he speak: and he shall declare unto you the things
that are to come.

Jesus understood that the apostles must make
their own demonstration and could not lean on
Him. Therefore He directed them to the Holy Comforter or Holy Spirit, which is the law of God in
action and the one supreme teacher. Eventually this
Spirit leads us into all Truth. "One jot or one
tittle shall in no wise pass away from the law."
Justice and righteousness must be meted out. The
Holy Spirit is the Comforter or God's love in action, which like a mother guides and helps and
forgives all who seek her.

14 He shall glorify me: for he shall take of
mine, and shall declare *it* unto you. 15 All things
whatsoever the Father hath are mine: therefore said
I, that he taketh of mine, and shall declare *it* unto
you.

The Holy Spirit is the dispenser of divine substance, and all prosperity demonstrations are made
through Him. The widow's mite was more than the
gift of the rich because the widow had blessed it and
it was her all. It is not the size of the object but
the blessing behind it that counts. Like the little

children blessed by Jesus, the mite, being blessed, increases mightily.

16 A little while, and ye behold me no more; and again a little while, and ye shall see me. 17 *some* of his disciples therefore said one to another, What is this that he saith unto us, A little while, and ye behold me not; and again a little while, and ye shall see me: and, Because I go to the Father? 18 They said therefore, What is this that he saith, A little while? We know not what he saith. 19 Jesus perceived that they were desirous to ask him, and he said unto them, Do ye inquire among yourselves concerning this, that I said, A little while, and ye behold me not, and again a little while, and ye shall see me? 20 Verily, verily, I say unto you, that ye shall weep and lament, but the world shall rejoice: ye shall be sorrowful, but your sorrow shall be turned into joy. 21 A woman when she is in travail hath sorrow, because her hour is come: but when she is delivered of the child, she remembereth no more the anguish, for the joy that a man is born into the world. 22 And ye therefore now have sorrow: but I will see you again, and your heart shall rejoice, and your joy no one taketh away from you.

The Christ always goes into the secret place by Himself in order to hold for greater strength and illumination, and when He attains this strength and illumination He comes out and demonstrates what He has received from the Father. Our thoughts get panicky and don't understand, and each time the Christ withdraws in order to receive new inspiration from God they are sorrowful; but when He comes forth and demonstrates, their sorrow is turned into joy. Ultimately they will come into the light of

Truth and understand what the indwelling Christ demonstrates when He goes into the silence to renew His strength. This is also true of the individual who is trying to "put on Christ."

Spiritual perception reveals to us that we are not persons but ideas in the cosmic Mind.

Jesus knew that the hour for His crucifixion was approaching. Crucifixion means the giving up of the whole personality. This was the demonstration that the Master was facing. However, He knew His spiritual power, and He was well aware that He would rise from the dead, would again be with His disciples, and would be more able than ever to instruct them in the mysteries of Being. "I will see you again."

23 And in that day ye shall ask no question. Verily, verily, I say unto you, If ye shall ask anything of the Father, he will give it you in my name. 24 Hitherto have ye asked nothing in my name: ask, and ye shall receive, that your joy may be made full. 25 These things have I spoken unto you in dark sayings: the hour cometh, when I shall no more speak unto you in dark sayings, but shall tell you plainly of the Father. 26 In that day ye shall ask in my name: and I say not unto you, that I will pray the Father for you; 27 for the Father himself loveth you, because ye have loved me, and have believed that I came forth from the Father. 28 I came out from the Father, and am come into the world: again, I leave the world, and go unto the Father. 29 His disciples say, Lo, now speakest thou plainly, and speakest no dark sayings. 30 Now know we that thou knowest all things, and needest not that any man should ask thee: by this we believe that thou camest

forth from God. 31 Jesus answered them, Do ye
now believe? 32 Behold, the hour cometh, yea, is
come, that ye shall be scattered, every man to his
own, and shall leave me alone: and *yet* I am not
alone, because the Father is with me. 33 These
things have I spoken unto you, that in me ye may
have peace. In the world ye have tribulation: but
be of good cheer; I have overcome the world.

"In that day ye shall ask me no question" means
that the apostles would have unfolded to the point
where they would understand the laws of Spirit
and would be able to read out of the law for themselves.

The "dark sayings" refers to the darkened consciousness that cannot see the true light. But this
Scripture indicates that "the night is far spent, and
the day is at hand." The apostles are coming into
a great illumination and will be able to go direct to the Father for light and guidance and power.
Hitherto the apostles have been students. Now they
are to come into a consciousness in which they
can tap the great universal reservoir and receive
therefrom. They are to realize that Omniscience
knows all things, and they have only to unify their
consciousness with that of Omnipresence in order
to enter into the state where the true light leads
into perfect understanding.

(See John 14:12-14 for further interpretation.)

# John: Chapter 17

These things spake Jesus; and lifting up his eyes to heaven, he said, Father, the hour is come; glorify thy Son, that the Son may glorify thee: 2 even as thou gavest him authority over all flesh, that to all whom thou hast given him, he should give eternal life. 3 And this is life eternal, that they should know thee the only true God, and him whom thou didst send, *even* Jesus Christ.

IN THIS SCRIPTURE Jesus was asking of the Father as never before. To glorify means to magnify with praise, to enhance with spiritual splendor. to adorn. Jesus was asking for a full and complete unification of His consciousness with that of the Father. Jesus realized that He had been given all authority over the flesh. He was holding the realization not only for His own glorification but also for that of His disciples. Jesus realized that in this union a full understanding of God and His laws would be revealed, which would naturally make clear to Him the way of eternal life.

4 I glorified thee on the earth, having accomplished the work which thou hast given me to do. 5 And now, Father, glorify thou me with thine own self with the glory which I had with thee before the world was. 6 I manifested thy name unto the men whom thou gavest me out of the world: thine they were, and thou gavest them to me; and they have kept thy word. 7 Now they know that all things whatsoever thou hast given me are from thee: 8 for the words which thou gavest me I have given unto them; and they received *them,* and knew of a truth that I came forth from thee, and they believed

that thou didst send me. 9 I pray for them: I pray
not for the world, but for those whom thou hast
given me; for they are thine: 10 and all things that
are mine are thine, and thine are mine: and I am
glorified in them. 11 And I am no more in the
world, and these are in the world, and I come to
thee. Holy Father, keep them in thy name which thou
hast given me, that they may be one, even as we *are*.
12 While I was with them, I kept in thy name
which thou hast given me: and I guarded them, and
not one of them perished, but the son of perdition;
that the scripture might be fulfilled. 13 But now I
come to thee; and these things I speak in the world,
that they may have my joy made full in themselves.
14 I have given them thy word; and the world
hateth them, because they are not of the world,
even as I am not of the world. 15 I pray not that
thou shouldest take them from the world, but that
thou shouldest keep them from the evil *one*. 16
They are not of the world, even as I am not of the
world. 17 Sanctify them in the truth: thy word is
truth. 18 As thou didst send me into the world, even
so sent I them into the world. 19 And for their
sakes I sanctify myself, that they themselves also
may be sanctified in truth. 20 Neither for these only
do I pray, but for them also that believe on me
through their word; 21 that they may all be one;
even as thou, Father, *art* in me, and I in thee, that
they also may be in us: that the world may believe
that thou didst send me. 22 And the glory which
thou hast given me I have given unto them; that
they may be one, even as we *are* one; 23 I in them,
and thou in me, that they may be perfected into one;
that the world may know that thou didst send me, and
lovedst them, even as thou lovedst me. 24 Father, I
desire that they also whom thou hast given me be
with me where I am, that they may behold my glory,
which thou hast given me: for thou lovedst me be-

fore the foundation of the world. 25 O righteous
Father, the world knew thee not, but I knew thee;
and these knew that thou didst send me; 26 and I
made known unto them thy name, and will make it
known; that the love wherewith thou lovedst me
may be in them, and I in them.

Jesus must have been the product of a former
cycle of time, and He had previously made the
perfect union in the invisible with the Father.

In proportion as people understand and have
faith in Jesus as their actual Saviour from sin,
and in proportion as they are set free from ap-
petite, passion, jealousy, prejudice, and all selfishness, they experience wholeness of mind and body
as the result. The ultimate result of this knowledge
and of daily practice in overcoming (even as Jesus
Himself overcame) will be a new race that will
demonstrate eternal life—the lifting up of the whole
man—spirit, soul, and body—into the Christ consciousness of oneness with the Father. This is indeed true glorification. By means of the reconcilia-
tion, glorification, and at-one-ment that Jesus re-
established between God and man we can regain
our original estate as sons of God here upon earth.

To comprehend this glorification requires a
deeper insight into creative processes than the av-
erage man and woman have attained, not because
they lack the ability to understand but because they
have submerged their thinking powers in a grosser
thought stratum. So only those who study Being
from the standpoint of pure mind can come into an
understanding of the transfiguration and of the part

that Jesus played in opening the way for humanity to enter into the glory that was theirs before the world was formed.

In its highest form, prayer is an exalted state of consciousness in which self-interest is lost in the desire to do good to everybody. Jesus always prayed the unselfish prayer. There are as many kinds of prayer as there are people in the universe. Those who pray for some personal good have no conception of the ecstasy of those who utterly forget self in their supplications for the good to be given to others. Yet all kinds of prayers are fulfilled. "Ask whatsoever ye will, and it shall be done unto you."

Those who spend much time in the Spirit come to be so much in love with it that they find it hard to endure the selfishness of the world, which they are tempted to leave entirely. Mystics and spiritual adepts withdraw to caves and the wilderness, as far from the haunts of men as they can get, because of the evil they see and feel so vividly. Then it becomes a real struggle to keep the self in the world. It is not right for one who has found this divine Truth within himself to withdraw from those who are ignorant of it and enjoy his riches alone. We should not think of being taken out of the world, but rather should we strive to keep our faculties from evil.

When we have found our being in God, we are no longer identified with the world; our interest is in spiritual things, and all our prayers are lifted up. "They are not of the world, even as I am not of the world." Through our intense realization of the eternal good and our unity with it we become so saturated with the thought of good that we are impregnable to evil. Thus we find that the doctrine of sanctification is based on Truth, and that it is possible for us to become so good in purpose that everything we do will turn to good. But we must certainly sanctify ourselves in Christ and persistently send forth the word of purity and unselfishness to every faculty in order to demonstrate it. We must not confine our prayer for perfection to ourselves alone but make it for them also that believe on Christ "through their word."

The realization of divine unity is the highest that we can attain. This is true glory, the blending and merging of the whole being into Divine Mind. "I in them, and thou in me, that they may be perfected into one."

This merging of God and man does not mean the total obliteration of man's consciousness but its glorification or expansion into that of the divine. This is taught in Hindu philosophy as the absorption of the soul into Nirvana, which has been erroneously interpreted as the total loss of individual consciousness instead of its majestic expansion.

# John: Chapter 18

When Jesus had spoken these words, he went forth with his disciples over the brook Kidron, where was a garden, into which he entered, himself and his disciples. 2 Now Judas also, who betrayed him, knew the place: for Jesus oft-times resorted thither with his disciples. 3 Judas then, having received the band *of soldiers,* and officers from the chief priests and Pharisees, cometh thither with lanterns and torches and weapons.

THE NAME KIDRON means "turbid stream." Kidron represents the current of confused thoughts that sometimes pour in upon us when we try to go into the silence. The "garden" locates the current in the world of universal thought. But this is a small matter compared with the activity of the great personal self in the subjective consciousness, Judas, who "knew the place," and took advantage of its darkness to capture the I AM. He came with a "band" (combative thoughts) and "officers from the chief priests and the Pharisees" (the idea of priestly authority and religious guidance from the standpoint of the letter), bearing "lanterns and torches and weapons" (light of the intellect, the torch of reason, and the force of circumstances).

Judas, representing the life principle, at this phase of overcoming is not fully redeemed from carnal thoughts and desires.

When Jesus went "over the brook Kidron" and entered the garden of Gethsemane, He passed in His own consciousness from the without to the within.

4 Jesus therefore, knowing all the things that were coming upon him, went forth, and saith unto them, Whom seek ye? 5 They answered him, Jesus of Nazareth. Jesus saith unto them, I am *he.* And Judas also, who betrayed him, was standing with them. 6 When therefore he said unto them, I am *he,* they went backward, and fell to the ground. 7 Again therefore he asked them, Whom seek ye? And they said, Jesus of Nazareth. 8 Jesus answered, I told you that I am *he;* if therefore ye seek me, let these go their way: 9 that the word might be fulfilled which he spake, Of those whom thou hast given me I lost not one. 10 Simon Peter therefore having a sword drew it, and struck the high priest's servant, and cut off his right ear. Now the servant's name was Malchus. 11 Jesus therefore said unto Peter, put up the sword into the sheath: the cup which the Father hath given me, shall I not drink it?

For the moment the personal will (the officers and soldiers, the executors of man-made laws) is here overcome. The second question is of the personality and milder. Jesus realizes that the time has come for Him to prove that the principles of almighty God are invulnerable and must stand. The I AM faced the condition unafraid (Jesus representing the I AM, answered, "I am *he*").

Your faith in the righteousness of your cause (Peter) may lead you to combat the ruling religious thoughts, and in your impetuosity you resent their counsel (Malchus, counselor) and deny their capacity to receive Truth (cut off the right ear); but good judgment and a broad comprehension of the

divine overcoming through which you are passing
will cause you to adopt pacific means. "Put up the
sword into the sheath."

"The cup which the Father hath given me" is
the consciousness of eternal life. This must be attained by a crucifixion, an utter "crossing out,"
of the personal self, both on its objective and subjective planes of volition; hence "they led him to
Annas" that other processes of the divine law might
be carried out.

> 12 So the band and the chief captain, and the
> officers of the Jews, seized Jesus and bound him, 13
> and led him to Annas first; for he was father in law
> to Caiaphas, who was high priest that year. 14
> Now Caiaphas was he that gave counsel to the Jews,
> that it was expedient that one man should die for
> the people.

"The band and the chief captain, and the officers
of the Jews" are found in the intellectual realm, and
it is before this tribunal that the Christ appears, to
be tested and tried. Annas was a leading factor in the
persecutions at the time of the ministry and crucifixion of Jesus. He represents intellectual opposition to spiritual Truth. His son-in-law Caiaphas, the
high priest, represents a ruling religious thought
force that is also entirely intellectual. He belongs
to the religious world of forms and ceremonies, the
"letter" of the word. The ruthlessness of these men
shows how a merely formal religion will persecute
and attempt to kill the inner Christ Spirit and all
that pertains to it.

15 And Simon Peter followed Jesus, and *so did* another disciple. Now that disciple was known unto the high priest, and entered in with Jesus into the court of the high priest; 16 but Peter was standing at the door without. So the other disciple, who was known unto the high priest, went out and spake unto her that kept the door, and brought in Peter. 17 The maid therefore that kept the door saith unto Peter, Art thou also *one* of this man's disciples? He saith, I am not. 18 Now the servants and the officers were standing *there,* having made a fire of coals; for it was cold; and they were warming themselves: and Peter also was with them, standing and warming himself.

Simon Peter followed Jesus, and so did another apostle. Simon Peter (symbolizing the faculty of faith) and the "other disciple" (John, symbolizing love) always sustain and support the I AM man in every trial.

19 The high priest therefore asked Jesus of his disciples, and of his teaching. 20 Jesus answered him, I have spoken openly to the world; I ever taught in synagogues, and in the temple, where all the Jews come together; and in secret spake I nothing. 21 Why askest thou me? ask them that have heard *me,* what I spake unto them: behold, these know the things which I said. 22 And when he had said this, one of the officers standing by struck Jesus with his hand, saying, Answerest thou the high priest so? 23 Jesus answered him, If I have spoken evil, bear witness of the evil: but if well, why smitest thou me? 24 Annas therefore sent him bound unto Caiaphas the high priest.

25 Now Simon Peter was standing and warming himself. They said therefore unto him, Art thou also

*one* of his disciples? He denied, and said, I am not.
26 One of the servants of the high priest, being
a kinsman of him whose ear Peter cut off, saith,
Did not I see thee in the garden with him? 27 Peter
therefore denied again: and straightway the cock
crew.

The high priest who questioned Jesus symbolizes a form of religious thoughts in man that
follows the set rule of the letter of the law with
little or no thought of its inner spiritual importance. Jesus (here representing the Christ) sets
forth the Truth in plain, concise language, which
however has no significance for the person functioning on the natural-religious plane of existence.

28 They lead Jesus therefore from Caiaphas into
the Prætorium: and it was early; and they themselves entered not into the Prætorium, that they
might not be defiled, but might eat the passover. 29
Pilate therefore went out unto them, and saith, What
accusation bring ye against this man? 30 They answered and said unto him, If this man were not an
evil-doer, we should not have delivered him up unto
thee. 31 Pilate therefore said unto them, Take him
yourselves, and judge him according to your law. The
Jews said unto him, It is not lawful for us to put
any man to death: 32 that the word of Jesus might
be fulfilled, which he spake, signifying by what
manner of death he should die.

The Praetorium symbolizes a state of despotism,
where force and cruelty and tyranny exist. The
Jews, symbolizing intellectual spirituality, would because of their religious traditions turn the Jesus
over to barbarians to be crucified.

The Jewish priesthood taught persecution as the unavoidable heritage of their race; even Jesus told His followers that they would suffer persecution when they taught His doctrine. At the age of thirteen a Jewish boy is considered a man ready to meet "persecution" and receives the blessing of the rabbi. Although it is true that the spiritual mind and the mortal are at war, metaphysicians see that the persecution of the Jews in every land is the result of the affirmation of the law of persecution by those with the power of the word. "Every idle word that men shall speak, they shall give account thereof."

33 Pilate therefore entered again into the Prætorium, and called Jesus, and said unto him, Art thou the King of the Jews? 34 Jesus answered, Sayest thou this of thyself, or did others tell it thee concerning me? 35 Pilate answered, Am I a Jew? Thine own nation and the chief priests delivered thee unto me: what hast thou done? 36 Jesus answered, My kingdom is not of this world: if my kingdom were of this world, then would my servants fight, that I should not be delivered to the Jews: but now is my kingdom not from hence. 37 Pilate therefore said unto him, Art thou a king then? Jesus answered, Thou sayest that I am a king. To this end have I been born, and to this end am I come into the world, that I should bear witness unto the truth. Every one that is of the truth heareth my voice. 38 Pilate saith unto him, What is truth?

And when he had said this, he went out again unto the Jews, and saith unto them, I find no crime in him. 39 But ye have a custom, that I should release unto you one at the passover: will ye therefore that I release unto you the King of the Jews? 40

They cried out therefore again, saying, Not this man, but Barabbas. Now Barabbas was a robber.

The Jews and the high priests and the officers who represent intellectual religious thought forces continued to work for Jesus' execution because they realized within their hearts that He was indeed a King, and they feared His spiritual power. The point to be considered by every follower of Jesus is His continued assertion that He is a King, right in the face of the desertion of His subjects and His imminent death; "a king! aye, a king! and every inch a king."

Barabbas was a prisoner charged with insurrection and murder. He was held at Jerusalem, and the Jews demanded that he be released instead of Jesus.

Metaphysically Barabbas represents the adverse consciousness (rebellion and hatred) to which man gives himself when he allows himself to oppose the Christ. Man gives free rein to this adverse consciousness when he would destroy the Christ or true spiritual I AM in himself, since it is through the Christ alone that an overcoming can be gained over the Adversary. This adverse state of thought (Barabbas) is of its father the Devil.

# John: Chapter 19

Then Pilate therefore took Jesus, and scourged him. 2 And the soldiers platted a crown of thorns, and put it on his head, and arrayed him in a purple garment; 3 and they came unto him, and said, Hail, King of the Jews! and they struck him with their hands. 4 And Pilate went out again, and saith unto them, Behold, I bring him out to you, that ye may know that I find no crime in him. 5 Jesus therefore came out, wearing the crown of thorns and the purple garment. And *Pilate* saith unto them, Behold, the man! 6 When therefore the chief priests and the officers saw him, they cried out, saying, Crucify *him,* crucify *him!* Pilate saith unto them, Take him yourselves, and crucify him: for I find no crime in him. 7 The Jews answered him, We have a law, and by that law he ought to die, because he made himself the Son of God. 8 When Pilate therefore heard this saying, he was the more afraid; 9 and he entered into the Prætorium again, and saith unto Jesus, Whence art thou? But Jesus gave him no answer. 10 Pilate therefore saith unto him, Speakest thou not unto me? knowest thou not that I have power to release thee, and have power to crucify thee? 11 Jesus answered him, Thou wouldst have no power against me, except it were given thee from above: therefore he that delivered me unto thee hath greater sin. 12 Upon this Pilate sought to release him: but the Jews cried out, saying, If thou release this man, thou art not Cæsar's friend: every one that maketh himself a king speaketh against Cæsar. 13 When Pilate therefore heard these words, he brought Jesus out, and sat down on the judgment-seat at a place called The Pavement, but in Hebrew, Gabbatha. 14 Now it was the Preparation of the passover: it was about the sixth hour. And he saith unto the Jews, Behold, your King! 15 They therefore cried out, Away with *him,* away with *him,* crucify him!

Pilate saith unto them, Shall I crucify your King?
The chief priests answered, We have no king but
Cæsar. 16 Then therefore he delivered him unto them
to be crucified.

17 They took Jesus therefore: and he went out,
bearing the cross for himself, unto the place called
The place of a skull, which is called in Hebrew
Golgotha: 18 where they crucified him, and with him
two others, on either side one, and Jesus in the midst.
19 And Pilate wrote a title also, and put it on the
cross. And there was written, JESUS OF NAZA-
RETH, THE KING OF THE JEWS. 20 This title
therefore read many of the Jews, for the place where
Jesus was crucified was nigh to the city; and it was
written in Hebrew, *and* in Latin, *and in* Greek. 21
The chief priests of the Jews therefore said to Pilate,
Write not, The King of the Jews; but, that he said, I
am King of the Jews. 22 Pilate answered, What I
have written I have written.

23 The soldiers therefore, when they had crucified Jesus, took his garments and made four parts,
to every soldier a part; and also the coat: now the
coat was without seam, woven from the top throughout. 24 They said therefore one to another, Let us
not rend it, but cast lots for it, whose it shall be: that
the scripture might be fulfilled, which saith,

They parted my garments among them,
And upon my vesture did they cast lots.

25 These things therefore the soldiers did. But there
were standing by the cross of Jesus his mother, and
his mother's sister, Mary the *wife* of Clopas, and
Mary Magdalene. 26 When Jesus therefore saw his
mother, and the disciple standing by whom he loved,
he saith unto his mother, Woman, behold, thy son!
27 Then saith he to the disciple, Behold, thy mother!
And from that hour the disciple took her unto his
own *home*.

28 After this Jesus, knowing that all things are

now finished, that the scripture might be accomplished, saith, I thirst. 29 There was set there a vessel full of vinegar: so they put a sponge full of the vinegar upon hyssop, and brought it to his mouth. 30 When Jesus therefore had received the vinegar, he said, It is finished: and he bowed his head, and gave up his spirit.

THE CONTEST FOR supremacy between the intellectual forces, represented by Pilate, and the pseudospiritual, represented by the Jews, is portrayed in John 19. Both contenders realize that it is a momentous occasion, and they seek to shift the responsibility for the destruction of the coming King Jesus and His rule. The rabble (sense consciousness) arrays Him in mock royal robes and a crown and cries, "Hail, King of the Jews!" Thus the sense man jeers at religion. To the ruling intellect Jesus has committed no wrong, and it beholds Him as a morally good man, saying, "Behold, the man!" When the Jews renew their cry of "Crucify him" because He claims to be the Son of God and a temporal ruler who is against Caesar, Pilate is troubled and appeals to Jesus, who replies that His rule is from above. When the Jews urge that Jesus is scheming to undermine and destroy Caesar's temporal rule Pilate becomes alarmed and calls a rehearing at Gabbatha (in Hebrew, a knoll or hill). We see at once that this signifies a high plane of human understanding.

Here Pilate (the intellect) again shifts the burden of rule to the Jews (the claimed spiritual authority) and says, "Shall I crucify your King?" The

Jews betray their allegiance to temporal things by
replying, "We have no king but Cæsar." The de-
cision to crucify Jesus was a combination of intellect
and pseudo Spirit and was carried out, as indicated,
by the co-operation of those taking part. "Then
therefore he [Pilate] delivered him unto them [the
Jews] to be crucified," and "the soldiers therefore
. . . crucified Jesus."

The Crucifixion took place at Golgotha, "The
place of a skull" (the front brain, the seat of the
will and conscious understanding, the throne of the
mind, where all ideas are tested and either enthroned or cast out). In the crucifixion of Jesus
both Pilate and the Jews (both the intellect and the
ruling spiritual ideas) unite in casting out the claim
that man is the Son of God. Although Jesus (representing the spiritual man) was not allowed to establish His conscious rule in the front brain, He
left a great unified doctrine of truth (represented
by the seamless garment that the soldiers found they
could not separate). So for two thousand years this
Truth has endured and is now being made king in
the conscious minds of those who believe. Before the
Son of God is enthroned the tables must be turned,
the intellect and the pseudospiritual must be crucified, and the great I AM elevated to the high place.

Jesus paid the supreme tribute to woman when
on the cross He recognized her and designated her
as the mother and preserver of love, to abide in the
home of His beloved disciple John.

Jesus became one of our human family for a purpose, to make it possible for us to attain spirit-

ual consciousness, which we could not do without the example of someone who had attained the goal. That we are sons of God is merely an idea until it has been demonstrated and enthroned in consciousness. Man is a child of evolution, the evolution of the perfect man implanted in us as by the Father-Mind. We were on the way to final demonstration of the Son of God when we lost our way in the delusions of sense. A guide and helper became absolutely necessary. Jesus assumed this dangerous and humiliating role. He had to become one of us in flesh and intellect, and it is this flesh-and-intellect man whose career is represented as being consummated in the offer of vinegar made to Him at His last human breath on the cross. So it was not Jesus the man of great ideas that was crucified; it was the flesh-and-intellect man, who cried out, "My God, my God, why hast thou forsaken me?"

31 The Jews therefore, because it was the Preparation, that the bodies should not remain on the cross upon the sabbath (for the day of that sabbath was a high *day*), asked of Pilate that their legs might be broken, and *that* they might be taken away. 32 The soldiers therefore came, and brake the legs of the first, and of the other that was crucified with him: 33 but when they came to Jesus, and saw that he was dead already, they brake not his legs: 34 howbeit one of the soldiers with a spear pierced his side, and straightway there came out blood and water. 35 And he that hath seen hath borne witness, and his witness is true: and he knoweth that he saith true, that ye also may believe. 36 For these things came to pass, that the scripture might be fulfilled, A bone of him shall not be broken. 37 And again another scrip-

ture saith, They shall look on him whom they
pierced.

The "Preparation" refers to the observances pre-
liminary to the celebration of the Jewish Sabbath,
or to the festival the day before the Sabbath. Among
the Jews there was a law to the effect that a lifeless
body should not remain upon the cross on the Sabbath, as this was a day set aside for rest and freedom from all troubled or contentious thoughts.
Hence Jesus' body was ordered removed.

The Jews asked that the legs of Jesus might be
broken and also those of the malefactors that were
crucified with Him. Crushing the bones destroyed
the last vestige of life in the body. Jesus appeared
to be dead, but the inference is that He still retained contact with the bone marrow from which
the blood or life is produced.

The fact that the demand of the Jews was not
executed shows the higher law was at work and not
a bone of Jesus' body was broken. The Scripture
prophecy was carried out even to the piercing of His
side, the place nearest the heart, the abode of love.

This whole Scripture reveals how those established in the intellect will seek to kill out the Christ,
and also how they are ultimately defeated in His
victory over death.

38 And after these things Joseph of Arimathea,
being a disciple of Jesus, but secretly for fear of the
Jews, asked of Pilate that he might take away the
body of Jesus: and Pilate gave *him* leave. He came
therefore, and took away his body. 39 And there came

also Nicodemus, he who at first came to him by night, bringing a mixture of myrrh and aloes, about a hundred pounds. 40 So they took the body of Jesus, and bound it in linen cloths with the spices, as the custom of the Jews is to bury.

41 Now in the place where he was crucified there was a garden; and in the garden a new tomb wherein was never man yet laid. 42 There then because of the Jews' Preparation (for the tomb was nigh at hand) they laid Jesus.

Jesus rested in the tomb of Joseph of Arimathea. Arimathea represents an aggregation of thoughts of lofty character, a high state of consciousness in man. Joseph represents a state of consciousness in which we increase in character along all lines. We not only grow into a broader understanding but we also increase in vitality and substance. Jesus' resting in Joseph's tomb symbolizes the truth that Jesus was resting in the consciousness of vitality and substance, was growing into a broader understanding, and was in truth gathering strength for the great demonstration over death to follow.

# John: Chapter 20

Now on the first *day* of the week cometh Mary Magdalene early, while it was yet dark, unto the tomb, and seeth the stone taken away from the tomb. 2 She runneth therefore, and cometh to Simon Peter, and to the other disciple whom Jesus loved, and saith unto them, They have taken away the Lord out of the tomb, and we know not where they have laid him. 3 Peter therefore went forth, and the other disciple, and they went toward the tomb. 4 And they ran both together: and the other disciple outran Peter, and came first to the tomb; 5 and stooping and looking in, he seeth the linen cloths lying; yet entered he not in. 6 Simon Peter therefore also cometh, following him, and entered into the tomb; and he beholdeth the linen cloths lying, 7 and the napkin, that was upon his head, not lying with the linen cloths, but rolled up in a place by itself. 8 Then entered in therefore the other disciple also, who came first to the tomb, and he saw, and believed. 9 For as yet they knew not the scripture, that he must rise again from the dead. 10 So the disciples went away again unto their own home.

11 But Mary was standing without at the tomb weeping: so, as she wept, she stooped and looked into the tomb; 12 and she beholdeth two angels in white sitting, one at the head, and one at the feet, where the body of Jesus had lain. 13 And they say unto her, Woman, why weepest thou? She saith unto them, Because they have taken away my Lord, and I know not where they have laid him. 14 When she had thus said, she turned herself back, and beholdeth Jesus standing, and knew not that it was Jesus. 15 Jesus saith unto her, Woman, why weepest thou? whom seekest thou? She, supposing him to be the gardener, saith unto him, Sir, if thou hast borne him hence, tell me where thou hast laid him, and I will take him away. 16 Jesus saith unto her, Mary. She

turneth herself, and saith unto him in Hebrew, Rabboni; which is to say, Teacher. 17 Jesus saith to her, Touch me not; for I am not yet ascended unto the Father: but go unto my brethren, and say to them, I ascend unto my Father and your Father, and my God and your God. 18 Mary Magdalene cometh and telleth the disciples, I have seen the Lord; and *that* he had said these things unto her.

ON THE RESURRECTION morning the friends and followers of Jesus seemed to have forgotten His promise that He would rise from the dead, and they looked for His body in the tomb. This incident shows that when the belief in death has overshadowed us, it darkens our understanding; we must pass from under this cloud before we can be conscious of the presence of awakened life. Mary was searching for her Lord and Master in the tomb even while He was at her side. John and Peter, failing to find Him where they expected Him to be, "went away again unto their own home."

Don't look in the tomb for the one you loved. Spirit is not confined in the chambers of the dead. When we fail to realize the new life in Christ we are sorrowful indeed. It is then that we should turn back to Christ Jesus (the I AM) who stands nearby and who says to the soul, "Why weepest thou? whom seekest thou?" Grief and the search for the lost one in some external place are then done away with quickly. The ascending thought of the I AM is the saving idea. "I ascend unto my Father and your Father, and my God and your God."

A resurrection takes place in us every time we thus rise to a realization of the perpetual indwelling life that connects us with the Father. We leave in the tomb of matter the graveclothes of mortal sense (the sense of being mortal), which are thoughts of man's limitation and inevitable subjection to material laws. Material laws are the laws that man has made for himself and his world.

The I AM is Spirit, but in order to rise into the realm of pure ideas it must not be attached to the clinging affections of the soul. (Jesus said to Mary, "Touch me not.") The two angels, "one at the head, and one at the feet, where the body of Jesus had lain," represent the positive words of life that bring spiritual powers to bear that lift the body out of matter into Spirit. These two bright and shining powers are possessed of animated intelligence as they say to the weeping Mary: "Why seek ye the living among the dead? He is not here, but is risen."

The most effective consolation that we can give to those who are immersed in the grief of separation and loss is to deny for them the human belief in death and affirm in thought, word and citations of Scripture the omnipresence of life. This dissipates the flood of sorrow thoughts that submerges the souls of those who mourn. Jesus did not want the sorrowing Mary thought to touch Him. The spiritual mind does not grieve; it does not look to matter and the limitations of the flesh for life eternal, and it dissipates the thoughts of sorrow by a denial of their reality or power to affect the mind of the Son of God.

Always keep to your highest thoughts and deny every suggestion of sorrow or loss. The children of darkness wear sackcloth and sit in ashes, but the children of light rejoice, look up ("ascend" in every thought to the Father of life and light), and are set free thereby from the burden of grief and from belief in death and separation.

19 When therefore it was evening, on that day, the first *day* of the week, and when the doors were shut where the disciples were, for fear of the Jews, Jesus came and stood in the midst, and saith unto them, Peace *be* unto you. 20 And when he had said this, he showed unto them his hands and his side. The disciples therefore were glad, when they saw the Lord. 21 Jesus therefore said to them again, Peace *be* unto you: as the Father hath sent me, even so send I you. 22 And when he had said this, he breathed on them, and saith unto them, Receive ye the Holy Spirit: 23 whose soever sins ye forgive, they are forgiven unto them; whose soever *sins* ye retain, they are retained.

Christianity began with Jesus Christ, was carried on by the apostles and the Seventy whom Jesus sent out two by two; then by other persons as they came into an understanding of Truth. This process of Christianizing will continue until the entire race is redeemed from error. Even so, as our faculties, our senses, and our thoughts learn the truth, they in turn give light and life to the thoughts that are still in darkness. In this way the entire man becomes established in immortality, eternal life.

Jesus Christ commissioned His followers to make disciples of all nations. This commission was given to them on a mountain in Galilee. A mountain always symbolizes spiritual elevation or a high place in consciousness. When the spiritually awakened and spiritually taught faculties and thoughts assemble with the I AM in spiritual consciousness, they are sent throughout the entire man, to the very outermost parts of the body consciousness.

In order to make the world Christian individuals must become Christian. The Christ Spirit must enter everyone. The Christ is knocking at the door of every heart, and He will enter when He is invited to come in. The mind that is open to Truth invites Christ to enter. When all men are filled with the Christ consciousness, international law will embody the Christ standard and the Christ kingdom will be established in the earth.

24 But Thomas, one of the twelve, called Didymus, was not with them when Jesus came. 25 The other disciples therefore said unto him, We have seen the Lord. But he said unto them, Except I shall see in his hands the print of the nails, and put my finger into the print of the nails, and put my hand into his side, I will not believe.

26 And after eight days again his disciples were within, and Thomas with them. Jesus cometh, the doors being shut, and stood in the midst, and said, Peace *be* unto you. 27 Then saith he to Thomas, Reach hither thy finger, and see my hands; and reach *hither* thy hand, and put it into my side: and be not faithless, but believing. 28 Thomas answered and said unto him, My Lord and my God. 29 Jesus saith unto him, Because thou hast seen me, thou hast believed: blessed *are* they that have not seen, and *yet* have believed.

30 Many other signs therefore did Jesus in the presence of the disciples, which are not written in this book: 31 but these are written, that ye may believe that Jesus is the Christ, the Son of God; and that believing ye may have life in his name.

Thomas is the apostle of Jesus who represents the understanding faculty of the natural man. Understanding and will function or should function in unison; each has its center of activity in the front brain, the forehead.

Among the apostles of Jesus Thomas stood for the head, representing the reason and intellectual perception. Jesus did not ignore Thomas's demand for physical evidence of His identity but respected it. He convinced Thomas by corporeal evidence that there had been a body resurrection and that it was not a ghost body that he saw but the same body that had been crucified, as was evidenced by the wounds that Thomas saw and felt.

The peace of Jesus came through the knowledge that there is no reality in death but that life is from everlasting to everlasting. He had proved His power to overcome the last enemy, death, and therefore He was established in "the peace of God, which passeth all understanding."

Jesus manifested Himself to the Eleven, and He upbraided them for disbelieving the accounts of His resurrection. Apparently the resurrection of Jesus is a great mystery, and to those who read the Bible in the letter and have no discernment of the power of Spirit to transform the body it must remain a mystery. The question often is asked whether or not we believe that Jesus rose from the dead with the same flesh body in which He walked the earth and, if so, what became of that body.

In former times believers accepted it as a miracle and made no attempt to explain the law by which it was accomplished, but blind faith is not so popular in the church as it once was, and skeptics are more bold. The school of "high criticism" is openly attacking Bible occurrences that it cannot account for under natural law. Thinking people are seeking a comprehensive explanation of the so-called miracles of the Bible. They wish to know how Jesus did His mighty works, including the resurrection of His body. The historical account makes clear that the flesh body that had been crucified was the body that Jesus had after His resurrection.

That Jesus knew how to restore life to dead organs is evidenced by His healing of paralytics, blind people, and in three cases by raising those who had died. He knew a way of restoring life that others living in His age did not know. He tried to explain it to His disciples and companions, but they did not understand. He told them that He would come to life again, but they seemed to have no comprehension of what He was saying. They thought He was talking to them about the Temple at Jerusalem, but He was talking of His body temple, which He could lay down and take up at will.

It is not at all surprising that the very near friends of Jesus were filled with astonishment and fear when they found that He was not in the tomb where they had laid Him. They could not understand that for years He had been training His soul to accomplish this very thing. He had spent whole nights in prayer, and through the intensity of His devotions had made union with Divine Mind. This union was so full and so complete that His whole being was flooded with spiritual life, power, and substance and the wisdom to use them in divine order. In this manner He projected the divine-body idea, and through it His mortal body was transformed into an immortal body. This was accomplished before the Crucifixion, and Jesus knew that He had so strengthened His soul that it would restore His body, no matter how harshly the body might be used by destructive man.

Jesus had obtained power on the three planes of consciousness: the spiritual, the psychical, and the material. After His resurrection He held His body on the psychical and the astral planes for forty days, and then translated it to the spiritual, where it exists to this day as a body of ethereal substance directed and controlled by His thought and mind force. Having a body of spiritually electrified atoms, Jesus is able to quicken the bodies of people who attract His presence by believing in Him; He radiates a glorious life that energizes those who believe in His power.

By positive affirmations we must all appropriate this same Christ life, substance, and Truth as ours individually and as the very foundation and substance of our body.

Thousands in this day have found the law that Jesus demonstrated and the inner meaning of the

Truth that He taught. They are working, praying, denying, affirming, concentrating, willing. They are in all ways building up the perfect-idea body, transforming flesh corruptible into substance incorruptible. Thus they are following Jesus in the regeneration. When they have renewed every organ and every part both within and without, and have put away all evidences of old age, the world at large will begin to accept their claims as true: that the destiny of all men is to transform the body of flesh into a body of Spirit and thus immortalize it. In this manner death is to be overcome and the earth made the dwelling place of immortal men.

This process of revealing and making use of the hidden forces of nature has already begun in the use of electricity, the radio, X rays, radar, and other invisible energies. The discovery that the atom has an electrical center was the first scientific break into omnipresent spiritual life. This life will be exploited by men until they exhaust the capacity of the machines they build to utilize it; then they will look for more efficient agents, which they will find in the development of the human body. Man's body directed by his mind is the only dynamo that can generate life and control it. Men can now build machines that smash the atom and liberate its latent forces, but the released energy can destroy the machinery and even the bodies of those who set it free.

Nature has within her all the elements necessary to the construction of heaven here on the earth and in the ether surrounding the earth. It won't be long before we shall be constructing houses in the air, but we must first learn how to levitate our body, as did Jesus; then resurrection will be part of our spiritual evolution and we shall know experimentally what Jesus meant by His death and resurrection, also just where He lives at the present time and what is required of us before we can meet Him in the heavens.

# John: Chapter 21

After these things Jesus manifested himself again to the disciples at the sea of Tiberias; and he manifested *himself* on this wise. 2 There were together Simon Peter, and Thomas called Didymus, and Nathanael of Cana in Galilee, and the *sons* of Zebedee, and two other of his disciples. 3 Simon Peter saith unto them, I go a fishing. They say unto him, We also come with thee. They went forth, and entered into the boat; and that night they took nothing. 4 But when day was now breaking, Jesus stood on the beach: yet the disciples knew not that it was Jesus. 5 Jesus therefore saith unto them, Children, have ye aught to eat? They answered him, No. 6 And he said unto them, Cast the net on the right side of the boat, and ye shall find. They cast therefore, and now they were not able to draw it for the multitude of fishes. 7 That disciple therefore whom Jesus loved said unto Peter, It is the Lord. So when Simon Peter heard that it was the Lord, he girt his coat about him (for he was naked), and cast himself into the sea. 8 But the other disciples came in the little boat (for they were not far from the land, but about two hundred cubits off), dragging the net *full* of fishes. 9 So when they got out upon the land, they see a fire of coals there, and fish laid thereon, and bread. 10 Jesus saith unto them, Bring of the fish which ye have now taken. 11 Simon Peter therefore went up, and drew the net to land, full of great fishes, a hundred and fifty and three: and for all there were so many, the net was not rent. 12 Jesus saith unto them, Come *and* break your fast. And none of the disciples durst inquire of him, Who art thou? knowing that it was the Lord. 13 Jesus cometh, and taketh the bread, and giveth them, and the fish likewise. 14 This is now the third time that Jesus was manifested to the disciples, after that he was risen from the dead.

WHEN THE DISCIPLES had toiled all night in their fishing boats without results, Jesus suddenly appeared on the shore and called to them, "Cast the net on the right side of the boat, and ye shall find." The result was 153 large fishes, so heavy that the net could not be lifted into the boat, yet it did not break. Man's mind is the net that catches thoughts, which are the basis of external conditions. The sea is the mental realm in which man exists. Toil of all kinds is a combination of mental and physical exertion. When the mind is exalted toil is easy. By using his mind man invents machinery that relieves him from wearying muscular labor. In a larger way the spiritual man uses his mind and takes advantage of divine guidance to lighten his toil.

The net of man's thought works hard and long in the darkness of human understanding and gains but little, but once the Christ Mind is perceived and obeyed the net is cast on the "right side," and success follows. The "right side" is the side on which man realizes the truth that inexhaustible resources are always present and can be made manifest by those who exercise their faith in that direction.

Whoever seeks supply through Spirit and submits his cause to the law of justice and righteousness always succeeds. The reason why men fail to demonstrate the many promises of divine support is that they cling to some selfish or unjust thought. "Seek ye first his kingdom, and his righteousness; and all these things shall be added unto you."

The bread and fish that Jesus provided on the

shore represents the supply of Spirit for the needs of the body. Not only does the Father provide for man in the natural world, as by the draught of fishes, but in the invisible world of substance are elements that correspond to the material things. Bread symbolizes the substance of the omnipresent Christ body and fish the capacity of increase that goes with it. Fish are the most prolific of all living things and aptly exemplify the ability of increase inherent in the Christ substance.

15 So when they had broken their fast, Jesus saith to Simon Peter, Simon, *son* of John, lovest thou me more than these? He saith unto him, Yea, Lord; thou knowest that I love thee. He saith unto him, Feed my lambs. 16 He saith to him again a second time, Simon, *son* of John, lovest thou me? He saith unto him, Yea, Lord; thou knowest that I love thee. He saith unto him, Tend my sheep. 17 He saith unto him the third time, Simon, *son* of John, lovest thou me? Peter was grieved because he said unto him the third time, Lovest thou me? And he said unto him, Lord, thou knowest all things; thou knowest that I love thee. Jesus saith unto him, Feed my sheep. 18 Verily, verily, I say unto thee, When thou wast young, thou girdest thyself, and walkedst whither thou wouldest: but when thou shalt be old, thou shalt stretch forth thy hands, and another shall gird thee, and carry thee whither thou wouldest not. 19 Now this he spake, signifying by what manner of death he should glorify God. And when he had spoken this, he saith unto him, Follow me. 20 Peter, turning about, seeth the disciple whom Jesus loved following; who also leaned back on his breast at the supper, and said, Lord, who is he that betrayeth thee? 21 Peter therefore

seeing him saith to Jesus, Lord, and what shall this man do? 22 Jesus saith unto him, If I will that he tarry till I come, what *is that* to thee? follow thou me. 23 This saying therefore went forth among the brethren, that that disciple should not die: yet Jesus said not unto him, that he should not die; but, If I will that he tarry till I come, what *is that* to thee?

24 This is the disciple that beareth witness of these things, and wrote these things: and we know that his witness is true.

25 And there are also many other things which Jesus did, the which if they should be written every one, I suppose that even the world itself would not contain the books that should be written.

Three times Jesus asked Simon Peter, "Lovest thou me?" Peter's spiritual advancement hinged on his possession of love, and the test of love is its willingness to serve. It is quite evident that Jesus was trying to teach Peter that if he loved truly he would serve.

Faith must be established in love and must work by love; and every faculty of man must be established in love and work by love if perfect harmony and good are to be realized. Faith established in love and working by love will remain steadfast at all times, under all circumstances; it will be our sustaining power during our every hour of need.

In verse 18 of this chapter Jesus explains further what He meant by His questioning. Faith (Peter), when it first begins to awaken to the Christ ideal, sees the unlimited possibilities that are presented in this new life; it realizes that it can bring into manifestation anything that may be desired. In its more mature state it realizes the necessity for service in a universal sense. The giving up of the personal self (with the consequent working from a universal standpoint) is the death whereby we are to glorify God. However, laying hold of Spirit and its power should accompany the denial of self.

Faith (symbolized by Peter) is the faculty on which depends continuous supply; hence Peter is challenged with the thought of love toward Christ three times. Faith must be in loving communion with the Christ Mind in order to draw down to the thoughts (sheep) the necessary supply. Man does not live by bread alone but by words and thoughts from God. These come into consciousness through mental and spiritual laws. Peter's three successive affirmations of love represent fulfillment of the close Christ union in spirit, soul, and body. Faith at the beginning is wistful, vigorous, vacillating, but in its maturity it gives itself wholly to Spirit and is willing to die to self. This is the "manner of death" by which faith glorifies God: being absorbed into the Divine Mind.

Through repeated affirmations of love toward Christ, man develops a consciousness of divine love that abides at the heart center and fills the whole body with ecstasy. This consciousness is "the disciple whom Jesus loved."

Jesus revealed the mind of the Father. This mind is the life and intelligence of man as well as the substance that provides for all his needs. This providing power of the Father, Jesus brought out prominently, and He showed in various ways how easy it is to obtain supply by trusting God. This teaching is not an encouragement to man to be idle, but rather to be active and trustful, constantly looking to Spirit instead of matter as the source of his good.

The actual resurrection of Jesus in a body that corresponds to the physical is not a subject open to debate by the followers of Jesus Christ. The historical evidence is ample to convince any unprejudiced mind. However, the study of the constituent parts of man, his spirit, soul, and body, reveals man's innate capacity to overcome the disintegrating effects of error thinking and living, and his ability, by conforming to the standards laid down by Jesus, to destroy the seeds of death and implant health and eternal life in his body.

To the oft-repeated question "If Jesus resurrected His physical body why is He not visible here among us?" we would say that Jesus overcame the sins that caused our original fall from the perfect body of the Adamic man to the diseased and dying body in which the race is now existing. When we have purified our mind and body and cast out every evil thought, our body will become transparent to human sight, as is Jesus' body. The idea that a transparent body is thin air, a ghost, is wholly wrong. Science says that the invisible electrical units composing the atom are millions of times more powerful than any visible thing. When the atomic energy in the atomic bomb was released great cities were destroyed. Jesus told His followers that when they were gathered in that upper room in Jerusalem the

Holy Spirit would descend upon them with power; and they were transformed from ignorant men into linguists of unbelievable ability.

Paul says, "Be ye transformed by the renewing of your mind." When we accomplish this transformation we shall see Jesus as He is and as we must all be in the resurrection from the dead and dying body in which we are now functioning. This is not to be accomplished by a great miracle at some appointed time in the future, but day by day we shall be resurrected out of the darkness of sense into the glorious light of Spirit.

# Question Helps

*for students of*

# Mysteries of John

## Chapter 1

1. What is the original creative word or *logos?*

2. Explain why the Word and the divine creative process are identical.

3. What is the metaphysical significance of the Book of John?

4. Explain the parallel between Genesis and John in relation to the ideal man.

5. What does John the Baptist represent?

6. What is the nature of the rock upon which Jesus built?

7. What is the true light?

8. How do we become children of God?

9. When was the "Christ or Word" incorporated into man's being?

10. Why are receptivity and belief essential?

11. How does the Word become flesh?

12. What is meant by "The law was given through Moses"?

13. Explain the statement "Grace and truth came through Jesus Christ."

14. Compare discernment with intellectual perception.

15. Explain the office of "baptism through denial, plus forgiveness" in the regenerative process.

16. Why is the recognition of oneself as the "Son of God" of primary importance?

17. What does baptism by John the Baptist symbolize?

18. What is the nature of the Father-Mind?

19. What is the function of the Holy Spirit?

20. How is the spiritual mind cultivated?

21. What mental attitudes are necessary to "put on Christ"?

22. What is the result of conscious recognition of the Christ Mind?

23. What quality does Andrew represent? Why is it important?

24. What is the metaphysical significance of Philip, Andrew, and Peter's being of the city of Bethsaida?

25. Why is it wise to develop the faculty of imagi-

nation under the direction of Spirit?

26. What does Bartholomew represent?

27. What is "consciousness"? "Form"?

28. What spiritual faculty is necessary for penetrating into the "fourth dimension."

## *Chapter 2*

1. What is the spiritual interpretation of marriage? Of Mary? Of Eve? Of Jesus? Of the disciples?

2. What does the name *Cana* mean? *Galilee? Philip?*

3. What mind activities are involved in the process of regeneration?

4. Give the inner meaning of "waterpots."

5. Explain "I, if I be lifted up . . . will draw all men unto myself."

6. What does the marriage in Cana of Galilee symbolize? Give the symbolism of this miracle in detail.

7. What does Capernaum designate?

8. What does the Passover symbolize?

9. Name the steps taken in body cleansing. Why must we deal with the mind in both the absolute and the relative?

10. Symbolically what is "the Christ light"?

11. How is a thought atmosphere produced?

12. Explain Paul's admonition "Think on these things."

13. What is the result of man's mastery of mind?

14. When is the word of God fulfilled in man?

15. Is Truth self-evident?

## *Chapter 3*

1. What does Nicodemus stand for in individual consciousness?

2. What is the "new birth"?

3. What are the steps in evolution?
4. How is permanent peace to be established?
5. How is man restored to the heavenly state?
6. What does believing in Jesus do for man?
7. How do we become like Jesus Christ?
8. How do we experience salvation?
9. What is represented by Jesus? By Judea? Metaphysically interpreted, what is the relationship of Jesus and John the Baptist?

## *Chapter 4*

1. What does Samaria represent? Sychar?
2. Where is "Jacob's well" situated?
3. Interpret metaphysically Jesus' resting by Jacob's well.
4. How does one worship God truly?
5. What is the spiritual significance of Jesus' journey from Judea to Galilee?
6. What is the "well of water springing up unto eternal life"?
7. Is the subconscious the true source of wisdom? Why do you answer as you do?
8. What is the symbology of the Samaritans' being regarded as pretenders by the Israelites?
9. From what sources does the soul draw its life? What is the ultimate source?
10. What is the explanation of spiritual things on a material basis?
11. In what way is Christ the discerner of thoughts?
12. Explain metaphysically the relation between Jews and Gentiles.
13. Jesus met the Samaritan woman by Jacob's well. Interpret.
14. Distinguish between intellectual reasoning and Spiritual perception.
15. Differentiate between the outer symbol of wor-

ship and worship in Spirit.

16. Is spiritual substance omnipresent? Explain.

17. Why is God no respecter of persons?

18. Why is it important for man to apprehend the laws of Spirit?

19. Why is absent healing possible? Give an instance of such healing.

20. What is the result when we attain oneness with the spiritual forces that move the mind?

## *Chapter 5*

1. What does Jerusalem represent?

2. Metaphysically interpreted, what is a feast in Jerusalem?

3. What do sheep symbolize?

4. Interpret spiritually the Pool of Bethesda and its five porches.

5. Why is the work of Spirit not confined to physical activities?

6. Why does divine life take no cognizance of intellectual laws?

7. What is the place in demonstration of the "sabbath of the Lord"?

8. What is the living power back of all nature?

9. Is the divine creative power continually alive?

10. Explain the relationship between the Father and the Son.

11. How does one honor the Christ?

12. Should one exercise wisdom in handling the life one has? Why?

13. What is the process involved in "raising the dead"?

14. Explain the relationship between judgment and love.

15. Why can one not successfully substitute the

Scriptures for the living Word?

16. How did Jesus create?

17. Why is the Bible not the living Word of God?

## *Chapter 6*

1. Why is it important to have an understanding of soul anatomy and the mind centers in the body?

2. Explain the nature of the I AM.

3. What part do the spiritual faculties have in the activity of the I AM?

4. How does one learn to live by the "living bread"?

5. What is the spiritual significance of Jesus and His disciples' going to the mountain?

6. Why did Jesus withdraw "into the mountain himself alone"? What is the significance of this for us today?

7. Explain the relationship between faith and power in one's walking "upon the waves of life."

8. What is the nature of the true source of substance?

9. Explain the interpretation of the Almighty as El Shaddai.

10. What process is involved in bringing spiritual substance into manifestation?

11. What is meant by the "last day"?

12. What is the nature of the body of Christ?

13. What is the true inner self of every individual?

14. How does one form one's environment, one's heaven or hell?

15. How do words become active in the body?

## *Chapter 7*

1. Why did Jesus' disciples want Him to go up to Jerusalem?

2. What human limitation of His ability to demonstrate did Jesus experience?

3. Explain the difference between the Pharisaical

mind and the spiritual mind.

    4. What effect does the outpouring of the Holy Spirit have within the soul?

    5. What is the procedure for handling a mixed state of consciousness?

    6. What is symbolized by the chief priests and officers?

    7. What does Nicodemus' spiritual conversion prove?

## Chapter 8

    1. What is represented by Jesus' going up to the Mount of Olives?

    2. What bearing does the story of the woman taken in adultery have on our own unfoldment?

    3. Explain the Scripture "I am the light of the world: he that followeth me shall not walk in the darkness, but shall have the light of life."

    4. How does man hinder his soul unfoldment? How can he accelerate it?

    5. Why must man abide in the Truth?

    6. How does man gain freedom? What part does concentration play in the quest of freedom?

    7. What is the result of ancestor worship?

    8. How does man bind himself to race beliefs regarding ancestry? How can he free himself?

    9. What is a liar and the "father" of all lies?

    10. Explain Jesus' words "Before Abraham was born, I am."

    11. Interpret the three parts in the Trinity? What is the "word"?

    12. Why were Jesus' words so powerful?

    13. Can man overcome death? Does this include death of the body?

## Chapter 9

    1. What is the general theme of John 9?

    2. Distinguish between the tents and tabernacles in

which the Israelites lived and Solomon's Temple.

3. Explain why the sin of omission is greater than the sin of commission?

4. What is man's real work?

5. What is the significance of the clay placed upon the blind man's eyes? Of its being washed away?

6. Explain the reaction that sometimes follows the activity of the "Jews" and "Pharisees" in consciousness?

## *Chapter 10*

1. What are the sheep mentioned in John 10? The "thief and a robber"? The porter? The "good shepherd"?

2. What part does man's own volition play in his reformation?

3. What is the result when the higher and lower forces are "married"?

4. What is the legitimate "door" through which spiritual energy enters man's consciousness?

5. What does Solomon's Porch symbolize?

6. How can a person be sure he is listening to the "still small voice"?

7. Metaphysically interpreted, what is the significance of Jesus' activity near the Jordan?

## *Chapter 11*

1. What does the name *Lazarus* mean? What does Lazarus represent?

2. What happens when man fails to recognize God as the origin and support of his life? What is the remedy for such a condition?

3. Describe one of the first steps in body restoration.

4. In what way does affirming life for another help one to overcome death?

5. Why do people grow old?

6. How is the "stone" rolled away?

7. Why is it important to give thanks for the manifestation even before it appears?

8. Explain why Jesus "cried with a loud voice."

9. Does the mind always accept Truth without question?

10. Explain the symbology of Jesus' withdrawal into Ephraim.

11. What does the Feast of the Passover represent?

## *Chapter 12*

1. What do we mean by the "fruit" of our thought?

2. What is the metaphysical significance of Mary's and Martha's serving Jesus?

3. What is symbolized by the anointing of Jesus' feet by Mary?

4. How does sense consciousness betray man?

5. How does love heal?

6. Are "signs" something to be desired for their own sake?

7. How is equilibrium restored?

8. "We lose our life in the service of the good." Explain.

9. What was Jesus' mission on earth?

10. Explain why Jesus had no real cause for worry.

11. What is represented by the multitude referred to in verse 34?

12. What state of consciousness results when the "Pharisaical intellect" rules?

13. Where does the preponderance of power in man lie? What is the true glory of man?

## *Chapter 13*

1. Can man live unto himself alone? Justify your answer.

2. How did sin come into the world? How is it cast out? How did Jesus become the universal Saviour?

3. How can man appropriate His life essence and repay Jesus for His great sacrifice?

4. What is soul unfoldment? How did Jesus teach it?

5. How does one become truly great?

6. Discuss the symbology of Jesus' washing His apostles feet.

7. How can one help mankind cleanse their understanding?

8. Why did Judas betray Jesus? Why did Jesus permit the betrayal?

9. What is true glorification?

10. Upon what spiritual quality does the preservation of Christianity depend?

## Chapter 14

1. Explain the relationship between the Father and the Son.

2. Explain "I go to prepare a place for you." Why did Jesus use the word "mansions"?

3. How does man find the Father? How does the Father principle operate?

4. What faculty does Philip represent? How does this faculty attain its highest expression?

5. What is the cause of and remedy for man's failure to demonstrate?

6. Why is attention so vital in sustaining our spiritual relation to the Father?

7. Where is the Spirit of truth? How is it brought into active touch with our consciousness?

8. Explain the Scripture "Ye behold me: because I live, ye shall live also" and "In that day we shall know that I am in my Father, and ye in me, and I in you."

9. In what sense is the individual man all that Jesus claimed He was? How does he make it manifest?

10. How does Jesus manifest Himself to us today?

11. What is the nature and character of the "personality" of the Holy Spirit?

## *Chapter 15*

1. Explain the relation of Jesus to the Father.
2. Why must man make intelligent use of his talents and faculties?
3. Explain how the power of the word functions through the I AM.
4. When does man cease to strive in external ways?
5. Give the method used to establish command over the real forces of Being.
6. Why did Jesus call the apostles "friends"?
7. Name the functions of the Holy Spirit.

## *Chapter 16*

1. What is the cause of persecution?
2. Why was it expedient for Jesus to go away?
3. What is your conception of the Holy Spirit?
4. Jesus said, "A little while, and ye behold me no more; and again a little while, and ye shall see me." Elucidate.
5. In reality what is man?
6. What in consciousness is "the crucifixion"?
7. Jesus said, "In that day ye shall ask me no question." Clarify.
8. In terms of mind what are "dark sayings"? Interpret "The night is far spent, and the day is at hand"?

## *Chapter 17*

1. For what was Jesus asking when He said, "Glorify thy Son, that the Son may glorify thee"? For whom did He pray?
2. When had Jesus made union with the Father?
3. To what extent does one experience wholeness of mind and body?
4. What soul attitudes are necessary to the production of the new race?

5. Explain why man must change the basis of his thinking from a grosser plane to that of pure mind.

6. Does God always answer prayer? What is the highest form of prayer?

7. What attitude of mind is involved in selfless prayer?

8. What is sanctification? What is its result?

9. What is man's highest attainment?

10. Discuss obliteration of individual consciousness versus expansion of the soul?

## Chapter 18

1. What does Kidron symbolize? Garden?

2. Interpret the action of Judas in the garden of Kidron.

3. What action is indicated by Jesus' passing over the brook Kidron?

4. Are spiritual forces invulnerable?

5. In what way are faith and love helpful in overcoming?

6. Distinguish between Truth and the letter of the law.

7. Explain the statement "Every idle word that men shall speak, they shall give account thereof."

8. What is the remedy for the state of consciousness represented by Barabbas?

## Chapter 19

1. What is the general theme of John 19?

2. Why does the sense man jeer at religion? What is the spiritual significance of arraying Jesus in royal robes?

3. What is indicated by Pilate's vacillating attitude?

4. Metaphysically explained, why was it necessary for Pilate and the Jews to co-operate in crucifying Jesus?

5. What is symbolized by Jesus' seamless robe? In what way is this symbol helpful today?

6. Discuss Jesus' great purpose in becoming one of the human family?

7. Was spiritual man crucified on the cross? Explain.

8. What in consciousness is "the Preparation"?

9. What is the lesson taught in John 19:31-37?

10. What is symbolized by Jesus' resting in the tomb of Joseph of Arimathaea?


## Chapter 20

1. What is the inner meaning of Mary's looking into the tomb?

2. Explain the Scripture "I ascend unto my Father and your Father, and my God and your God."

3. What is the significance of Jesus' words "Touch me not"? What do the two angels represent?

4. What is the most effective way to comfort the bereaved? Does spiritual mind ever grieve?

5. What influence does the individual Christian have upon the race?

6. What does Thomas symbolize?

7. How is the "peace of God, which passeth all understanding" acquired?

8. Why is spiritual discernment necessary in understanding the Resurrection? Is the raising of Jesus' flesh body a "mystery"?

9. Explain something of the law by which the Resurrection was accomplished.

10. On what three planes of consciousness did Jesus develop power?

11. How does Jesus quicken the bodies of men today? How does man co-operate with Jesus in the regeneration?

12. How does man immortalize his body? In what way is science helpful in the regeneration?

13. Is the resurrection of man's flesh body a part of spiritual evolution?

## *Chapter 21*

1. Of what is the net symbolic? The sea?

2. What is the spiritual significance of casting the net on the "right side"?

3. Why does man sometimes fail to demonstrate substance?

4. Discuss the symbology of the bread and fishes on two planes of consciousness.

5. What lesson was Jesus teaching when He asked, "Lovest thou me"? Why must love go hand in hand with faith and the other faculties?

6. Explain the inner meaning of verse 18.

7. In what way may the "manner of death" be said to glorify God?

8. Metaphysically what is the "disciple whom Jesus loved"?

9. What two attributes of the "mind of the Father" are necessary in claiming one's good?

10. How may we "destroy the seeds of death" and implant health and eternal life in the body?

11. Why is the resurrected body of Jesus not visible today? How can man follow Jesus' example?

12. Paul said, "Be ye transformed by the renewing of your mind." Explain.

# INDEX

# INDEX

# About the Author

Charles Fillmore was an innovative thinker, a pioneer in metaphysical thought at a time when most religious thought in America was entirely orthodox. He was a lifelong advocate of the open, inquiring mind, and he took pride in keeping abreast of the latest scientific and educational discoveries and theories. Many years ago he wrote, "What you think today may not be the measure for your thought tomorrow"; and it seems likely that were he to compile this book today, he might use different metaphors, different scientific references, and so on.

Truth is changeless. Those who knew Charles Fillmore best believe that he would like to be able to rephrase some of his observations for today's readers, thus giving them the added effectiveness of contemporary thought. But the ideas themselves—the core of Charles Fillmore's writings—are as timeless now (and will be tomorrow) as when they were first published.

Charles Fillmore was born on an Indian reservation just outside the town of St. Cloud, Minnesota, on August 22, 1854. He made his transition on July 5, 1948, at Unity Village, Missouri, at the age of 93. To get a sense of history, when Charles was eleven, Abraham Lincoln was assassinated; when Charles died, Harry Truman was President.

With his wife Myrtle, Charles Fillmore founded the Unity movement and Silent Unity, the international prayer ministry that publishes *Daily Word*. Charles and Myrtle built the worldwide organization that continues their work today, Unity School of Christianity. Through Unity School's ministries of prayer, education, and publishing, millions of people around the world are finding the teachings of Truth discovered and practiced by Charles and Myrtle Fillmore.

Charles Fillmore was a spiritual pioneer whose impact has yet to be assessed. No lesser leaders than Dr. Norman Vincent Peale and Dr. Emmet Fox were profoundly influenced by him. Dr. Peale borrowed his catchphrase of *positive thinking* from Charles Fillmore. Emmet Fox was so affected by Fillmore's ideas that he changed his profession. From an engineer, he became the well-known writer and speaker.

Charles Fillmore—author, teacher, metaphysician, practical mystic, husband, father, spiritual leader, visionary—has left a legacy that continues to impact the lives of millions of people. By his fruits, he is continuously known.

Printed U.S.A.                                  38-3336-3M-3-97